Employability

Insights from Chinese and British Universities

Troy Heffernan
Weizhe Feng
Robert Angell
Fang Yan
Dan Coxon

China Agricultural University Press

· Beijing ·

图书在版编目（CIP）数据

大学生就业力的需求与培养：中英比较研究 /（英）赫弗南（Heffernan, T.），冯伟哲
主编. —北京：中国农业大学出版社，2012.9
ISBN 978-7-5655-0590-4

Ⅰ.①大… Ⅱ.①赫… ②冯… Ⅲ.①大学生–职业选择–对比研究–中国，英国
Ⅳ.① G647.38

中国版本图书馆CIP数据核字（2012）第 208259号

书　　　名	Employability	
	Insights from chinese and British Universities	
作　　　者	Troy Heffernan　Weizhe Feng　Robert Angell　Fang Yan　Dan Coxon	

责 任 编 辑	童　云　田树君	封 面 设 计	James Drayson
出 版 发 行	中国农业大学出版社		
社　　　址	北京市海淀区圆明园西路 2 号	邮 政 编 码	100193
电　　　话	发行部 010-62818525,8625	读者服务部	010-62732336
	编辑部 010-62732617,2618	出 版 部	010-62733440
网　　　址	http://www.cau.edu.cn/caup	E-mail	cbsszs@cau.edu.cn
经　　　销	新华书店		
印　　　刷	涿州市星河印刷有限公司		
版　　　次	2012 年 9 月第 1 版　　2012 年 9 月第 1 次印刷		
规　　　格	787×1 092　　16 开本　　16.25 印张　　370 千字		
定　　　价	86.00元		

图书如有质量问题本社发行部负责调换

Special thanks must go to the two institutions which supported this research program. Plymouth University, UK and China Agricultural University helped resource and support this study; both institutions value the importance of developing employable graduates.

This book is an output from the PMI2 Project funded by the UK Department for Innovation, Universities and Skills (DIUS) for the benefit of the Chinese Higher Education Sector and the UK Higher Education Sector. The views expressed are not necessarily those of DIUS, or the British Council.

Cover design by James Drayson (www.jamesdrayson.com)

Foreword

The rapidly increasing numbers of students enrolling in the higher education system in the UK has necessarily prompted an institutional change towards a more specified and focused student experience, leading ultimately to the production of highly competitive graduates. Such competitive output is necessarily underpinned by an increased emphasis on employability at all levels of service delivery, from government policy on one hand through to HE staff development on the other hand. The shift towards employability focus coincides with a similar shift towards greater internationalisation in the sector, with both the UK and China rightly prioritising the enhancement of the overall student experience.

This book represents the culmination of a particularly successful collaboration between China Agricultural University in Beijing, and Plymouth University, UK. A strong partnership between two key institutions is fundamentally important for understanding the complex international issues present in the global education market, and for developing strategies to increase overall student competitiveness in a modern economy.

From my own perspective, this book forms an integral part of the growing literature examining the complexities involved in creating a holistic student package which continues long after graduation. The authors and contributors come from a wide range of backgrounds and bring extensive experience of the concept of employability in both China and the UK. Their experience is reflected in the friendly approach taken in the text, yet also in the detailed strategic practices that are reported.

It would be hard to understate the importance that enhancing employability has, and will continue to have, in the sector and texts such as this will be at the forefront of high impact academic and pedagogic dissemination.

Bill Rammell, 2012
Minister for Higher Education, 2005-2008
Deputy Vice-Chancellor for Internationalisation and the
Student Experience,
Plymouth University, 2011-2012

About the Authors

Professor Troy Heffernan

Professor Troy Heffernan is Director of International Partnerships at Plymouth Business School, Plymouth University. His pioneering research into transnational education has led to numerous invitations around the world to run workshops and presentations to enhance best practice in the field. Other research streams Dr Heffernan explores are lecturer effectiveness and student employability enhancement. His research-led approach to education has resulted in the development of a range of new programmes at Plymouth University. These have been commended for being innovative, recognising aspects of internationalisation and for embedding employability.  For his contributions to enhancing learning and teaching around the globe Dr Heffernan has received various awards including the Australia and New Zealand Marketing Educator of the Year (2004); and the University of Plymouth: Inspirational Teaching Award (2010). He has over 50 international publications, and has published in such journals as the Journal of Marketing Education and the Journal of Higher Education Policy and Management.

Professor Weizhe Feng

Professor Weizhe Feng received his MSc degree at the University of Reading, and PhD at China Agricultural University. He is the Deputy Dean of the International College Beijing. Professor Weizhe Feng has two main research specialisms. The first is international education, where he has published more than 20 research papers and 7 books. For his excellence in research achievements he received three government awards, including the National Second Class Award for Excellence in Education and Teaching Research (2009) given by Ministry of Education;

the Provincial First Class Award for Excellence in Education and Teaching Research (2008) given by the Beijing Municipal Government; and the Provincial Second Class Award for Excellence in Education and Teaching Research (2005) given by the Beijing Municipal Government. His second research area is ICT-based knowledge transfer and management. In this field he has published more than 20 research papers in academic journals, and has also received a Provincial Third Class Award for Social Science Research Achievement (2009), given by the Beijing Municipal Government.

Dr Robert J. Angell

Rob is a lecturer at the Cardiff Business School where he teaches research methods at undergraduate and postgraduate levels. He received his PhD in Marketing at the Plymouth University for a model applying a finite mixture structural equation model to the UK's older consumer population. Rob is a full member of the Market Research Society and has published in respected international journals such as the Journal of Business Research and Journal of Marketing Management.

Fang Yan

Fang Yan is a lecturer in Human Resource Management at International College Beijing, China Agricultural University. With a MSc in organisational and social psychology from the London School of Economics, she has consulted with internationally recognised multinational companies and taught several courses in organisational behavior and human resource related subjects. Her research interests include organisational behavior and human resource management in a dynamic global business environment.

Dan Coxon

Graduating from Plymouth Polytechnic in 1989 with a degree in Politics and Law and a passion for music, Dan was lucky enough to spend 20 years selling culture to the youth market. His move to the charitable sector shifted both his personal and professional emphasis, and here is where he started to work with young and emerging artists to help progress their careers.It was only when he joined academia as a Lecturer in Marketing at Plymouth Business School in 2010 that this work was given a context, and that was employability.Dan was Awarded Plymouth Business School 'Employability Champion' in 2011.Today Dan has returned to the charitable sector working at Young Devon a progressive charity committed to improving the

chances for young people. Dan continues to develop practical projects for young people to enhance their employability skills.

We would like to acknowledge the support and assistance of Kerryn Husk, Emma Heffernan, Hugh Conway, Hui Zhang and Lingyuan Meng in the research and delivery of this book. We are also grateful to the authors of the case studies: Lynne Hammond, Dave Burnapp, Ulrike Hillemann, Elaine Walsh, Christine White, Alison Oddey, Fan Xia, Sarah McNicoll and David Croot.

Contents

List of tables and figures

1 Introduction

Issues of employability have faced every generation of graduates, and the questions facing graduates today reflect the rapid expansion in scale experienced in recent years. In the 1980's, graduates who aspired to work in 'glamorous' industries faced the same challenges: how to stand out? Why should they get the job? In 2011, with increasing numbers of graduates entering the employment market each year, these questions have spread across all disciplines and the concept of employability has rightly become a focus at local, national and international levels.

In China, the escalation in higher education admissions for university programmes has led, unsurprisingly, to a situation where competition for jobs is fierce. At the same time evidence suggests that Chinese employers want more from graduates, particularly in terms of employability (Zhang, 2006; Venter, 2003). A key objective of reports such as the 2003-2007 Action Plan in China (State Council, 2004) was to increase the numbers of graduates entering the workplace with adequate skills for employability. More recently, in the Outline of National Middle and Long Term Education Development and Reform Plan (China Central Government, 2010), it was realised that "many students have limited capability in employability...Employment led education and teaching reforms are to be further initiated".

The same is true in the UK, where current research has indicated that employers have highlighted a lack of quality in graduates. There has been a rapid change in many fields meaning that discipline specific knowledge is not sufficient to produce highly employable individuals; such knowledge quickly becomes outdated. Skills development is therefore a central concern (Rundle-Thiele, Bennett and Dann, 2005).

Across the globe, the market for higher education is growing; as new global markets emerge and economic power relationships shift, governments around the world are recognising the importance of training a larger proportion of their workforces to university level and beyond. This is especially true of countries such as the UK and China, who are actively growing a workforce to operate in an emerging knowledge economy. In the UK there were upwards of 2.4 million students at higher education institutions during the academic year 2009/10, including more than 500,000 postgraduate students (Universities UK, 2011). Similarly, enrolments at Chinese universities grew from 3.2 million in 1997 to almost 15 million in 2005 (6Xue Info, 2008). These levels of university numbers make graduate competitiveness both an important and increasingly sizeable problem in both countries.

Table 1.1 UK graduate unemployment

Academic year	Employed(%)	Unemployed(%)
2009/2010	74.4	7.4
2008/2009	72.4	7.6
2007/2008	74.9	6.5
2006/2007	77.0	4.7
2005/2006	76.7	5.1
2004/2005	76.3	5.3

(HESA,2001)

In the UK, the Higher Education Policy Unit has seen graduate unemployment rise to 14% (December 2009); the highest recorded level. With 69 gradua-tes now competing for each job, universities must focus on the exit velocity of their students to ensure that they are best equip-ped to face the competitive wo-rld into which they emerge.

1.1 Employability

These increases in student enrolment numbers, alongside fierce employment competition, mean that employability has become a central concern for both universities and policy makers alike. A country's economic performance is directly linked to the construction and maintenance of a highly qualified and flexible workforce (Knight, 2001). The responsibility of training employees to fit into this global economy falls to higher education institutions. This importance is reflected in documents such as the Dearing Report in the UK; and the 2003-2007 Action Plans in China.

> *"The job market remains challenging for new graduates as it does for others. But a degree is still a good investment in the long term and graduates have a key role to play in helping Britain out of the recession."* (Rt Hon David Willetts MP, The Higher Education Minister)

The key features of these plans are to increase the numbers of skilled and employable graduates entering the job market. Agencies such as ESECT (the Enhancing Student Employability Coordination Team) in the UK, and the Ministry of Education for the People's Republic of China, are overseeing this aim. Employers in both the UK and China are increasingly dissatisfied by the quality of graduates entering work. The ESECT report *Learning and Employability* stated reasons for declines in national productivity and concluded that the failure of UK universities to develop graduates was central (Yorke, 2004). Similarly, in China it has been reported that employers are satisfied by the academic credentials of their graduates but are less pleased by the ability of recruits to demonstrate the key skills required to successfully move through the business (Zhang, 2006; Venter, 2003). Indeed, the term *'key skills'* has itself proven problematic because of a mismatch between how education providers and employers define and understand the concept (Holmes, 2001).

> *"Graduates face an extremely competitive employment market. However, a degree remains a valuable investment. [Russell Group] Universities are constantly striving to ensure that their students develop skills-sets that make them employable, entrepreneurial and experienced."* (Dr Wendy Platt, Director General, The Russell Group)

Consequently there is a need to enhance the employability of graduates at universities around the world; and it is within this context that the current volume has been written. The overarching aim of the book is to present the reader with a comprehensive understanding of the concept of employability, the components that make up employability and different ways and means of enhancement through the university experience. To achieve this, the book is divided into three sections; *theory and practice, empirical evidence and, lastly, case studies.*

The book is organised to logically and comprehensively explore all of these issues; firstly through a brief examination of education and the fundamental principles of employability, then a discussion of how employability should be implemented in H.E institutions. This implementation can take many forms, and student-centred as well as lecturer led fields are considered prior to an examination of how culture impacts on the learned experience. The methods, approaches and results of a primary research phase are detailed along with illustrative case studies exploring employability in differing settings.

More specifically, the first section, Section A, explores the emergence of the concept of employability; the components of employability, issues around embedding employability and student responsibilities surrounding their own employability. This section comprises four chapters:

2. Education and employability;

3. Implementing employability;

4. Student centred approaches to employability;

5. Culture, learning and employability.

The second section, Section B, identifies findings from a large empirical research project examining the employability attributes graduates require to succeed in industry; as deemed by employers in three different disciplines; marketing, accounting/finance and human resource management. Lecturers and other experts in the field of employability were consulted in order to determine strategies which enhance these attributes. The study was conducted in both the UK and China; allowing for different culturally based concepts of employability to emerge. Section B is divided into four chapters:

6. Methodology;

7. Results A: The marketing discipline and employability;

8. Results B: The accounting/finance discipline and employability;

9. Results C: The human resource discipline and employability.

The final section of this book, Section C, presents case studies exploring the different topics and strategies surrounding employability enhancement. The section presents an accurate account of the state of employability strategies entrenched in current university policies. Further, a number of these cases illustrate programmes that have been structured alongside Chinese universities; again allowing for elements of cultural difference to emerge. There are six chapters in Section C, each based on a single case study:

10. *Employability led course design: The development of the MSc Marketing Management & Strategy at Plymouth Business School;*

11. *Knowledge transfer in Higher Education; London College of Fashion;*

12. *Collaborative development of online modules concerning employability and entrepreneurship; University of Northampton;*

13. *Using summer school to develop the employability of PhD students; Imperial College London;*

14. *Entrepreneurship for the creative and media arts; Nottingham Trent University and Shanghai Institute of Visual Arts.*

15. *Enhancing employability through life-wide learning; Plymouth University*

Lastly, the sections are summarised and some tentative conclusions are posited in Chapter sixteen which outlines the similarities and differences between the employability situation in the UK and China. Additionally, the applicability to the wider literature is considered alongside the implications for both policy and individuals. These final sections conclude, unsurprisingly, that employability should be more fundamentally entrenched into all levels of higher education and that the strategies used to integrate these skills should be developed in conjunction with key graduate employers.

Enhancing students' employability is a critical concept for universities around the world to grapple with,as it is how universities change and adapt to this challenge that will be one of the key drivers for the sector in the future. The universities that enhance the student experience and deliver career-ready,employable graduates with a broad range of skills and competencies will be those that succeed in the new environment.

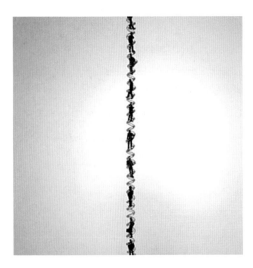

Section A: Employability – Theory and Practice

In recent years it has been well documented that modern higher education systems play an integral role in the development of national economies. A vital cog in the sustained growth of any economy is human capital,though in conjunction with scientific advancements, engineering, manufacturing and information technology related inventions and innovations. In the UK this position has been entrenched by the Labour Government of the late 1990s and their aspiration for fifty per cent of the population to attain a higher level qualification. This demonstrated a substantial change in the way in which university level education was delivered in the post-war era of the twentieth century. The UK was, at the time, similar to most other countries (e.g. USA, China etc.) in that far fewer people studied at degree level; vocational training was the predominant way into the national workforce. The vocational training route has been superseded by a modern higher education system and,as such, it has gradually become the role of the university providers to bridge the gap between further education and successful graduate employment. However in the UK at least, there has been a shift back towards vocational training with the reintroduction of apprenticeships.

2 Education and Employability

As outlined in the first chapter, in recent years, employability has become, in both the UK and China, a central aspect of higher education. Why should this be the case? It is this fundamental question which is addressed in this chapter through an examination of the development of higher education in the two countries. The concept of employability in its most general form is outlined,and the role of culture in the social world (and its influence on education) is introduced using evidence from the East and West.

2.1 Brief history of higher education(H.E)

The first university in the United Kingdom was Oxford, founded in the 12th Century. There followed five other universities in England and Scotland,and this total of six colleges remained until the nineteenth century when Durham, London, Manchester, Newcastle-upon-Tyne and the University of Wales were formed. Until well into the twentieth century, student numbers were low,and with education being considered a privilege, most of the universities accepted students from only the pre-requisite private schools. Attending university required the student to be wealthy; no loans, scholarships or state funding was provided. As the restrictions on education decreased, a number of new universities began to open and student numbers rose. In modern times, former 'polytechnic' colleges have been redefined and rebranded into university institutions (Green, 1999).

The University of Oxford was the UK's first university founded in 1167. At this time, British academics working at the University of Paris were in the process of being expelled from France. Choosing Oxford to settle back into the UK, the University of Oxford was subsequently formed.

Alongside Cambridge (jointly referred to as 'Oxbridge') Oxford remains a centre of excellence for education throughout the world.

In China, the first university can be traced back to 1306 in the Yuan Dynasty. Guozijian was organised to provide the schooling required for the family and friends of government officials, educating them in the areas of literature and governance. In more recent times, the first Chinese modern university, Jingshi Grand University (the former Peking University) was founded by the Qing Dynasty in 1898. Adopting both the traditional Chinese education and that from Japan, the US and Europe, the university consisted of a Chinese division and a western educational division. In the early 1920s, seven universities were established by the Chinese government and a further sixteen by Christian foundations. The Chinese educational system has continued to experience systematic growth; however, modern higher education in China suffered during the Cultural Revolution led by Mao Zedong.This ultimately led to the closure of universities during 1966-1976. Higher education was resumed after 1977 with the economic and social

reforms led by Deng Xiaoping;however, until the 1990's university level education remained a privilege and only conservative numbers of students were admitted onto courses (Shu, 1961; Chen, 1979).

Under the leadership of Mao Zedong, the Chinese Higher Education System closed for more than ten years to encourage a return to communism. Following Mao's death in 1976, the political, economic and educational reforms associated with the Cultural Revolution were terminated.

2.2 Rapid expansion of higher education

The integration of a number of former polytechnic colleges into university status institutions is indicative of the rapid expansion of H.E in the UK; the UK now has over 100 degree-awarding institutions. Student admissions have risen from 374,000 to 2.4 million since 2003 (Universities UK, 2008; 2011). This increase, it has been suggested, is the consequence of policies which originated under the conservative government of 1979-1997 (Oldfield and Baron, 2000). The commissioning of the Dearing Report by the Labour government in 1997 saw increasing attention drawn to the actual numbers in education. The report recommended a significant expansion of the system and Tony Blair, the (then) Prime Minister called for 'education; education; education.' Reflecting this, the UK Government set achievement rates of a 'one in two' attendance.

In October 2010 Lord Browne published a White Paper reviewing Higher Education provision and funding in the UK, and when implemented this report will fundamentally reshape the sector. Removing the limit placed on fees that universities can charge, the report's radical reappraisal of Higher Education Governance and funding allows for an increase of 10% in the numbers of university places available over the coming years (i.e. by 2013).

Table 2.1 Percentage of English domiciled students 1999-2006

Academic year	1999	2000	2001	2002	2003	2004	2005	2006
English Domiciled Students(%)	39	40	40	41	40	40	42	40

(HESA, 2011)

China's expansion of higher education, on the other hand came as a result of increased economic growth throughout the 1990s. During this period it became apparent that the development of higher education should be accelerated in order to cope with the large demand of human resources required in the 21st century (Mao, 2008). The Chinese government launched the "211" programme to enhance support for the top 100 universities in terms of funding; policies for the rapid expansion of enrolment numbers were put into place during 1999. Compared with the 1.08 million enrolments in 1998, admissions in 1999 soared to 1.53 million – a 48 percent increase. Since 1999, exponential growth has continued, and well into 2008 a total of 5.99 million new entrants were recorded, more than 5 times that of 1998 (Yuan, 2008; China Education Yearbook, 1976-2008).

Such escalation in higher education admissions for both undergraduate and postgraduate programs in both the UK and China has led, unsurprisingly, to a situation where competition for graduate jobs is fierce. At the same time evidence has suggested that employers want more from graduates in the UK (Yorke, 2004), and China (Zhang, 2006; Venter, 2003). It is this central issue which will be addressed in the following sections.

Key Points:

✓ **The Dearing Report in the UK and the "211" Programme in China have both been influential in the expansion of university education.**

✓ **Subsequently, both the UK and China have witnessed substantial growth in student admissions.**

✓ **This expansion inherently leads to increased competitiveness in the graduate job market.**

2.3 What is employability?

"A set of achievements, skills and understandings and personal attributes that make an individual more likely to gain employment and be successful in their chosen occupation which benefits themselves, the workforce, the community and the economy." (Prof Peter Jones, Senior Pro-Vice Chancellor, Nottingham Trent University, cited in CBI "Future Fit")

The majority of the literature dealing with employability refers to the Western world. Dating back to the start of the 20th Century, employability was first conceptualised (largely in the USA) to refer to the availability of able workers (deGrip et al., 2004). Unsurprisingly, this definition evolved greatly and since the 1960s has become a more personal term, outlining the qualitative and quantitative qualities which are present in job competition. At its broadest, however, employability is simply the ability to be employed (Hillage and Pollard, 1998).

Conceptualisations in the Chinese literature tended to imply the ability to gain *satisfactory* employment as integral to the definition of employability (Mu, 2006; Fang and Xie, 2006; Zheng et al., 2008). In this regard, the term is seen as the capacity of an individual to gain employment, maintain it and then to gain new employment when required. It is this perception in both countries that has instigated a wave of comparative studies (often between universities) which compare employment levels and make assertions about the employability of the graduates as a result. However, Brown et al. (2003) suggest that claims of this nature are inherently flawed, as employability and employment are by no means synonymous.

In their *'Employability: developing a framework for policy analysis'* (1998), Hillage and Pollard define employability as:

> *"...the capability to move self-sufficiently within the labour market to realise potential through sustainable employment."*

But simply being employable does not guarantee employment. In a more comprehensive sense, the definition supplied above is loaded and focuses on securing a first graduate job.It ignores the contribution that external factors have on the ability of a person to gain employment. These include the demand for labour at the time, the economic climate and the supply of skilled workers, to name only a few (Harvey, 1999). Evidence of this situational dependence is seen in China where the numbers of graduates exceed the supply of jobs available to them and competition is therefore fierce (Zhiwen and van der Heijden, 2008).

The ability to attain employment must be conceptualised as a two-sided process in which external and internal (i.e. the personal attributes of the employee) factors are the foundations. The disentangling of employability and employment has been a fairly recent development in the literature;with some arguing that the concept is more about an individual's capacity to do a particular job (Yorke, 2004), or whether one is equipped for a certain role (Harvey, 1999). More comprehensive definitions examine the holistic nature of learning experiences across all spheres (in the theme of Jackson's (2011:2) conception of "life-wideness"). The focus is therefore on personal qualities rather than the initial gaining of employment:

> *"Employability is the propensity of [post/graduates] to exhibit attributes that employers anticipate will be necessary for the future effective functioning of their organisation"* (Harvey, 1999: 100)

The most suitable definition for employability with all of these issues in mind, and the one utilised throughout the remainder of this book, is provided by the 2003 '*Enhancing Student Employability Coordination Team*' report, a definition also utilised by Gedye and Chalkley (2006):

> "...a set of achievements – skills, understandings and personal attributes – that make graduates more likely to gain employment and be successful in their chosen occupations, which benefits themselves, the workforce, the community and the economy".
> Enhancing Student Employability Coordination Team (ESECT), 2003:4

Many policy makers in the UK and China believe it to be the responsibility of higher education institutions to ensure that graduates demonstrate attributes considered salient by employers. The 1997 Dearing Report in the UK argued that training should provide a framework which enables competition on a global stage (NCIHE, 1997). As this view became integrated within systems thinking, students in the UK came to see a degree as only the final addition to their learning tool kit.

> "When you look at the people who are going to university they have been encouraged to think that education has given them employability skills, so as well as learning about history or English or business studies, they are also learning problem solving, developing communication skills, so they are pretty confident about themselves." Prof Kate Purcell, Warwick University Institute for Employment Research

An undergraduate degree is often mistakenly perceived by students as a guarantee of a well-paid position in the employment market; however often this is often not the case. A degree is simply not sufficient to ensure the career progression that many students, unused to failure throughout their preceding academic careers, expect. Those universities that focus their efforts on adding value across the learning experience are better equipping their graduates for the challenges which they face.

Similarly, the 2003-2007 Action Plan for China's educational system placed emphasis on the improvement of teaching methods and resources in universities. In the fourth of six projects within the action plan, it was stated that educational reforms should drive employment in the graduate sector. Consequently in both the UK and China it was felt that the university system should be the training stage for students making the transition into employment. Despite this some authors felt that such a focus was wasteful on the resources of institutions, as employers rarely utilise the skills they demand (Knight and Yorke, 2004). Nonetheless it is imperative that universities produce graduates with strong opportunities to find meaningful employment in the field that they choose, especially given the costs incurred during studying. It is the employment sector, rather than academia, which sets the criteria against which potential employees are measured; and so it is necessary to identify the specific attributes that employers desire from graduates.

2.4 Salient employability capabilities

The ESECT report 'Are your students employable' (2003), examined the important factors raised by employers as well as reflecting the work of Hawkins (1999) and Harvey (1997). The list of attributes consisted of 15 major salient points and provides an insightful, yet basic, view of current employability characteristics.

Table 2.2   A list of employability attributes

Attribute	Definition
Team Working	Ability to be an effective team leader, and to work effectively in more than one team
Leadership	Ability to take control of a situation and empower peers
Interpersonal Skills	Ability to relate to and feel comfortable with people at all levels, and maintain relationships
Customer Orientation	Ability to establish confident and flexible relationships with people important to the business
Communication	Effective communication – written and verbal
Foreign Language	Effective written and oral communication in more than one language

Table 2.2 Continued

Attribute	Definition
Self-Promotion Skills	The ability to advertise strengths – to sell
Networking Skills	The ability to build contacts
Action Planning	The ability to manage several tasks at once
Problem Solving	The ability to analyse data and to solve problems
IT Literacy	The ability to accommodate new technologies and make the most of their benefits
Flexibility	The ability to respond to change
Numeric Skills	The ability to gather statistical data
Business Acumen	The ability to use skills appropriate in a commercial environment
Understanding of commercial goals	An understanding of organisational values

(Source: adapted from ESECT, 2003)

Whilst these fifteen employability attributes have useful 'checklist' properties, other researchers have looked to integrate such single-dimensional attributes into multi layered models. The most influential study to incorporate this was undertaken in the UK by Knight and Yorke (2004), who proposed a four-part model referred to as USEM (Table 2.3). The authors suggested that their USEM model explains the characteristics displayed by *employable* graduates, and also recommend that the model be applied cross-nationally. The components of USEM are: (1) understanding, (2) skilful practices, (3) efficacy beliefs, and (4) metacognition. Table 2.3 provides a description of each component of the model and provides a list of the specific characteristics desired by employers.

Table 2.3 Components of the USEM model

Component	Description	Desired Characteristics
U Understanding of the subject	Propositional knowledge in the form of mastery of the subject matter of the degree	- Subject understanding - General understanding - Organisationalunderstanding - Enterprise
S Skillful practices	What are often called generic skills as well as subject specific skills. These can be characterised as procedural knowledge	- Organising - Interpersonal skills
E Efficacy beliefs	Belief that one generally can make some impact on situations and events. This dispositional element can be loosely interpreted to refer to other aspects of personality	- Motivation - Determination and commitment - Confidence - Assertiveness - Coping with stress
M Metacognition	Awareness of what one knows and can do, and how one learns more	- Learning to learn

(Source: Knight and Yorke, 2004)

2.5 What are employability skills?

"A set of attributes, skills and knowledge that all labour market participants should possess to ensure that they have the capability of being effective in the workplace – to the benefit of themselves, their employer and the wider economy." Confederation of British Industry

Across the spectrum of career opportunities the mix of skills required of graduates naturally varies between roles and between industries. The skills and attributes required to make an individual candidate employable in some professions will be different to those that would make them employable in others.

In the current UK climate of fragile recovery out of recession, where record numbers of graduates are entering the work market to compete with large numbers of unemployed graduates from previous years, students must develop a rounded package of skills related to the career path that they want to follow. Only in this way will they better equip themselves to be successful in their employment search. The top-level skills which will recur throughout this book, from personal development through to numeracy skills, are covered in depth in key texts such as Hind and Moss (2011). However, at this stage, what is central is the notion that these are often split into those skills which are discipline specific and those which are broader.

2.5.1 Discipline specific skills

Subject specific skills refer to the ability to 'do the job' and are sometimes termed 'hard skills'; and may include:

- Technical ability
- Knowledge
- Qualifications

Historically there has been an assumption among graduates that it is these discipline specific skills which are more central than broader employability skills. However in a rapidly developing knowledge economy, these become obsolete almost instantaneously and so it is the ability to access, network and communicate new information clearly which is vital to developing career success.

2.5.2 Broader employability skills

So called 'softer', broader scope skills were identified as largely fitting into the following areas (sourced through the Department of Education, Science and Training (DEST, 2005), the Australian Chamber of Commerce and Industry (ACCI) and the Business Council of Australia (BCA)):

Initiative

- Adapting to new situations
- Developing a strategic long-term vision
- Being creative
- Identifying opportunities not obvious to others
- Translating ideas into action
- Generating a range of options
- Initiating innovative solutions.

Communication

- Listening and understanding
- Speaking clearly and directly
- Writing to the needs of the audience
- Negotiating responsively
- Reading independently
- Empathising
- Using numeracy effectively
- Understanding the needs of internal and external customers
- Persuading effectively
- Establishing and using networks
- Being assertive
- Sharing information
- Speaking and writing in languages other than English.

Teamwork

- Working with people of different ages, gender, race, religion or political persuasion
- Working as an individual and as a member of a team
- Knowing how to define a role as part of a team
- Applying teamwork skills to a range of situations e.g. crisis
- Identifying strengths of team members
- Coaching, mentoring, and giving feedback.

Technology

- Having a range of basic IT skills
- Applying IT as a management tool
- Using IT to organise data
- Being willing to learn new IT skills
- Having the occupational health and safety knowledge to apply technology
- Having the appropriate physical capacity.

Problem Solving

- Developing creative, innovative solutions
- Developing practical solutions
- Showing independence and initiative in identifying problems and solving them
- Solving problems in teams
- Applying a range of strategies to problem solving
- Using mathematics including budgeting and financial management to solve problems
- Applying problem-solving strategies across a range of areas
- Testing assumptions, taking the context of data and circumstances into account
- Resolving customer concerns in relation to complex project issues.

Self-Management

- Having a personal vision and goals
- Evaluating and monitoring own performance
- Having knowledge and confidence in own ideas and vision
- Articulating own ideas and vision
- Taking responsibility.

Planning	Learning
• Managing time and priorities – setting timelines, coordinating tasks for self and others • Being resourceful • Taking initiative and making decisions • Adapting resource allocations to cope with contingencies • Establishing clear project goals and deliverables • Allocating people and resources to tasks • Planning the use of resources including time • Participating in continuous improvement and planning • Developing a vision and a proactive plan to accompany it • Predicting – weighing up risk, evaluating alternatives, applying evaluation criteria • Collecting, analysing, and organising information • Understanding basic business systems and their relationships.	• Managing own learning • Contributing to the learning community at the workplace • Using a range of mediums to learn – mentoring, peer support, networking, IT, courses • Applying learning to technical issues (eg, products) and people issues (eg, interpersonal) • Having enthusiasm for ongoing learning • Being willing to learn in any setting, on and off the job • Being open to new ideas and techniques • Being prepared to invest time and effort in learning new skills • Acknowledging the need to learn in order to accommodate change.

(Source: Australian Chamber of Commerce and Industry & Business Council of Australia, 2002)

In their report '*Ready to grow*: *business priorities for education and skills - Education and Skills Survey 2010*', The Confederation of British Industry (CBI 2010) highlighted the need for graduates to possess not only a good degree but also key additional skills. The survey identified a growing concern: 22% of employers were worried about graduates' limited career awareness. A further 39% felt that graduates should have more relevant work experience. Derived from these results, the CBI developed a clearer picture of the key employability skills sought by its members:

- *Self-management*: a readiness to accept responsibility, flexibility, time management, readiness to improve own performance;

- *Team working*: respecting others, co-operating, negotiating/ persuading, contributing to discussions;

- *Business and customer awareness*: a basic understanding of the key drivers for business success and the need to provide customer satisfaction;

- *Problem solving*: analysing the facts and circumstances and applying creative thinking to develop appropriate solutions;

- *Communication and literacy*: an application of literacy, ability to produce clear, structured written work and oral literacy, including listening and questioning;

- *Application of numeracy*: manipulation of numbers, general mathematical awareness and its application in practical contexts;

- *Application of information technology*: basic IT skills, including familiarity with word processing, spread sheets, file management and use of internet search engines.

In the Chinese literature there has been less agreement on what is meant by employability attributes. This reflects the little research which has been conducted in the field; that which does exist also tends to define the wider concept inadequately. Nonetheless, Table 2.4 outlines a study by Li, Liu, and Wong (2005) classifying 20 personal traits into three distinct categories:

Table 2.4 Classification of employability for graduates

Inner quality	Ability to deal with work	Social Skills
Honesty and integrity	Analysing and judging	Expression
Hardworking	Logical thinking	Leadership
Devoted to work	Problem solving	Social activity
Responsibility	Independence	Organising and co-ordination
Initiative	Adaptability	Interpersonal skills
Ambition	Ability to handle change	Entrepreneurship
	Learning	
	Team working	

(Source: Li et al., 2005)

The conceptualisations of employability discussed throughout this chapter represent a basic but useful framework for gaining a better understanding of the general skills and capabilities linked to employability. However whether or not these skills are wholly transferable across a wide variety of contexts (or industries) is yet to be established. Whilst they serve as evidence of research in the area, further empirical studies would clarify the key employability attributes needed across a variety of disciplines and countries.

SUM-UP

- ✓ 'Employability' is the skills and capabilities that make someone employable for a particular role.
- ✓ Employability skills can be taught via a number of mediums, but for them to be embedded within university courses is preferable – 'extra-curricular' activities are also advisable.
- ✓ The type of employability skills will probably differ between industries and jobs.

3 Implementing Employability

The previous chapter introduced the concept of employability skills and we will now consider how these are effectively delivered. Equipping students with the necessary skills and capabilities needed to successfully meet the requirements of the employment market is often understood to be the responsibility of higher education providers. Whilst it is likely that many skills are learned prior to joining university – particularly for mature students – the university is perceived to be the ideal outlet for developing the necessary capabilities en-route to full-time employment.

3.1 Blended integration

The integration of employability skills should be embedded across the breadth of the education sector, from placement activities through to inter-disciplinary exercises. Within this framework there are broadly two major spheres in which such skills can be acquired, the educational curriculum (from delivery to assessment) and students' participation in extra-curricular and alternative activities (Fallows and Steven, 2000). Historically (pre-1990), institutions tended towards a whole module dedicated to skills development, for example IT and communication skills. Alternatively material was delivered outside of the main curricula, particularly through university societies and clubs; indeed anything in which students collectively undertook tasks unrelated to their core course material.

The 1990s saw increasing understanding throughout UK institutions of the benefits employability skills provision could bring and therefore also saw a more holistic delivery of capability development. There are three main streams through which to embed such skills into learning material at individual, module and programme levels:

1. Attribute development in the programme of study through use of skills and/or internal work experience as part of the course;

2. Enhanced central support in skills development/search for potential

work;

3. Innovative provision of work experience outside of the course (part-time jobs, mandatory holiday study).

(Source: Harvey, 2005)

Additionally, Harvey (2005) argues, record keeping and reflexive activities personally administered by the student are beneficial, though delivery of these can also be at personal, module or institution level.

The situation in China is similar to that in the UK. Recent research indicates that Chinese H.E.I's have moved away from a solely 'career-guided' focus and towards an increasingly integrated appro-ach (Zeng, 2004). Whilst it is recognised that there are specific employability capabilities which should be integrated into university wide curricula, more emphasis is usually placed on the specific credits available for completion (Ministry of Education, 2008).

Key points:

✓ Graduates should develop employability skills and capabilities through a blend of curricular and extra-curricular activities.

✓ Alongside classroom based activities, being involved in events and organisations could be beneficial, eg: University sports societies, clubs or groups as well as part-time work or internships.

Personalisation of development is central to the ethos of most university led learning and the delivery of employability skills is no exception. The emphasis is therefore on the freedom of choice between distinct elements. Additionally, Chinese professors are engaging in a broad range of delivery methods and assessment techniques in order to further engage learners. In keeping with the modern turn in the blended technological delivery of material (utilising online and other methods), employability material can now take the form of case studies, seminars, online forums and similar (Liu et al., 2008). Outside of these delivery methodologies, students are also often required to participate in other academic and social activities, including conference attendance, report writing and presentations alongside more communal activities. In this sense more practical elements represent an important step in the delivery of a quality educational product (Wen, 2006). Many institutions have incorporated specialised modules which endorse these skills. Students' involvement will undoubtedly improve more transferrable skills and the development of communicative, creative and adaptive skills is certainly endorsed by the majority of Chinese universities (Liu and Zang, 2008; Wen, 2006).

Clearly, there are areas of similarity between the UK and China about how employability should be integrated into university level course structures; though a more central issue is the *procedural* elements of delivery for the necessary skills (Yorke and Knight, 2004). Strategies often employed, such as work-based learning or extended work-related courses can have detrimental impacts on other key skills. These methods are spread largely across undergraduate curricula which are necessarily longitudinal; whereas postgraduate courses tend towards shortened, more intensive delivery. Such differences highlight the need to differentiate integration according to the length and delivery structure of courses. The central feature of this differentiation is ensuring individuals do not 'miss-out' through course elective choices.

As an example, at the University of Luton, UK, employability was built into programmes by utilising core (mandatory) modules as vehicles for delivering the relevant skills, ensuring all students gained the necessary material (Fallows and Steven, 2000). Such integration is no easy task; the need to deliver not only the correct course material but the integrated skills of employability leaves course designers with significant technical and administrative challenges (Yorke and Knight, 2004). Simultaneously, educators are expected to maintain levels of consideration towards learners and the assessment criteria must, at the very least, be sympathetic. There is no 'one-size fits all' solution to the embedding of employability material into pre-existing modules and programmes; differing disciplines will have significantly different needs.

Material integration is certainly problematic, however its delivery, as stated, also poses interesting challenges. When developing employability for the programme-level, Fallows and Steven (2000) have argued that lecturing staff need opportunities to include local requirements. In the example of the University of Luton, lecturing staff were encouraged to place greater emphasis on employability through assessment practices, as well as delivery. The level of emphasis employed, and the state of the delivery, rested with the individual teaching member rather than the institution (Bloxham, 2005). These emphases depended largely on the discipline, staff member and student as well as the course material. It is crucial, however, that these important skills are evidenced and that courses are tailored to exhibit a balanced and proportional delivery which is not to the detriment of other skill sets (Yorke and Knight, 2004). A framework with associated course auditing procedures is therefore not a viable or desirable option; the discussion around integration of material highlights the dependence on multiple variables.

Some courses have developed specia-list modules devoted to employability. The University of Luton has seen good results from this approach. However, the success of modules depends grea-tly on a number of variables. This book does not aim to provide a framework for this type of provision, but does give potential strategies for teachers and decision makers to adopt in their own courses.

So far this chapter has considered the importance of employability and how it is conceptualised, as well as the process for implementing it in a university context. The remainder will explore three key themes: firstly, the impact of implementation itself will be considered; secondly, how employability increases in specificity with graduate level and; thirdly, some barriers to employability both in the UK and China will be discussed.

3.2 Implementing employability: enabling structures

The key focus of the implementation of employability skills should be lecturing staff. Whilst there are many spheres affecting the integration and application of these skills, it is the knowledge and dynamism of delivery staff which is central. Clearly these individuals do not work in isolation and even the most creative lecturer needs support and institutional processes in order to successfully deliver a learning environment that embeds employability with students.

The effectiveness of the delivery and integration of employability skills is necessarily linked to the delivery and integration of any material delivered to students and, therefore, the effectiveness of the lecturer becomes of central importance. Clear communication, delivery dynamism and assessment fairness all impact directly on teaching effectiveness (Sweeney et al., 2009). Thus it is these elements which impact most greatly on the delivery of employability skills to students entering the market. However, it is certainly not the case that lecturing staff operate (or have responsibility) in isolation, Figure 3.1 outlines the layers of supportive and integrated structures needed for the successful delivery of employability skills.

Figure 3.1 Integrative support structures

The lecturer (1) is necessarily at the forefront of employability skills delivery and it is the creative, inclusive and knowledgeable integration of these skills into their teaching which is the most effective way of ensuring a match between employer and graduate. These skills should therefore be built into the core outcomes of both modules (2) and programmes (3). There is little possibility of theoretically grounded and enthusiastic delivery by lecturing staff if the material does not form part of the indicative content of sessions.

However, in order for the material to be successfully integrated into any level there should be widespread and coherent support alongside recognition of the importance of employability skills from the wider faculty and department (4) – at managerial, administrative and strategic levels. Necessarily, this will be indicative of a wider university (5) focus on employability; the need for senior strategic staff alongside developmental and support structures to integrate these skills is hard to overstate.

In its broadest sense the impact of the wider national culture (6) on employability skills delivery is significant. Clear, concise and rigorous exchange of information between employers and universities would ensure that accurate information is delivered at all stages and, ultimately, lead to more employable graduates. At each stage, there should be a firm integration of employment needs into structures and processes – only then can the dynamic and creative delivery by lecturing staff have the greatest impact.

Clearly such a model is idealistic and cannot be thought to operate in a pure form in any real-world system; there are many and varied limiting factors. Examples in the UK of such limiting factors are the two-stage checking processes by which assessments are validated. Students' work is moderated internally, within a particular institution, and subsequently a representative percentage is moderated by an external examiner. Such a system contains significant inertia and potentially limits the elements of creativity which can be introduced by lecturing staff. As Sweeney et al. (2009) indicate, creative assessment directly impacts on teaching effectiveness and so limiting this dynamism will affect student uptake of employability information. Not only that, but the central features of teaching effectiveness identified by Heffernan et al. (2009) revolve around dynamism, rapport and communication. These are all naturally limited in a model which incorporates such assessment procedural elements as the UK system. Creativity in delivery, knowledge application and assessment are fundamental to the ideal integration of employability as dictated by the model proposed in this section.

At each stage, acceptance of the integration described by this layered typology would represent a step closer to fully integrated and accurate employability skills delivery. The actual design and incorporation of this material is down to individual course managers and teaching staff in association with employers – however there are some broad themes which emerge as important to delivery. It is to these that this chapter will now turn.

3.3 Multi-level application of employability skills sets

It is worth considering the differences in the level of capabilities expected from learners at different stages of the educational process. For example, are there significant differences between third-year undergraduate candidates aiming to obtain work placements, graduates and post-graduates?

Informal conversations with academics and experts in the field of employability indicated that students at differing stages are actually in a position to offer employers a remarkably similar product. However it is the employer's expectations which alter from graduate to post-graduate. In simple terms, as students' progress through the educational system they acquire more (and more specialised) employability capabilities at differing levels (see Figure 3.2). The level of specificity, as well as the level of integration, will increase the further an individual progresses through the system, leading to highly prepared postgraduates; prepared, that is, for a more competitive job market. In context, this highlights the important distinction between 'life-wide' and 'life-long' learning, both crucial to holistic approaches to employability (Jackson, 2011).

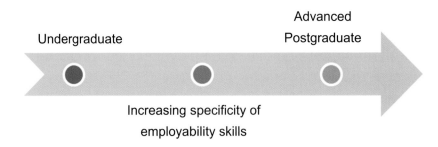

Figure 3.2 Employability skill and progression continuum

The identification of specific employability capabilities as designated by employers therefore becomes a central issue, alongside distinguishing between levels of graduate. The following sections will concentrate largely on the demands made upon graduates and postgraduates when searching for employment.

The increased specificity necessary in postgraduate work (when compared to graduate) should be embedded in the integration process by academics. However, at the same time, this delivery cannot logically be totally incorporated at all times and for all students. Thus, the level of implementation and the barriers to integration are also outlined over the following sections.

3.4 Barriers to employability

Increasingly, universities are required to deliver to the work-place well educated, well rounded and employable graduates across a broad range of disciplines. Whilst there are discipline specific integration characteristics, graduates themselves are not passive. Individuals must consider how best to equip themselves for the employment market and the challenges faced, for UK students at least, in times of austerity.

Individual students make these choices within the boundaries of a multi-level set of stakeholder conditions; each having limited but significant influence on the employability skills available. The following sets of figures illustrate these stakeholder conditions whilst also showing the continuum on which each lies. These continua demonstrate the range of attitudinal beliefs from completely integrated employability skills to more traditional beliefs, which hold that education is sufficient.

STUDENTS:

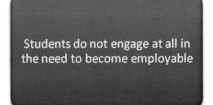

LECTURERS:

Lecture staff who believe a university is a centre for knowledge transfer Lecture staff recognise the need and are fully committed to including employability development in their programmes

COURSES:

Courses that are focused solely on the academic and knowledge transfer. Likely to lead to an academic or research career Courses that have a high level of employability embedded such as engineering, were the focus is on developing a career

UNIVERSITY MANAGEMENT:

Vice Chancellors and academic staff who believe the university is a seat of learning, and it is up to the student to take advantage of the opportunities available to them Vice Chancellors and academic staff who believe the university should be highly proactive in encouraging its students to be as employable as possible

UNIVERSITY ETHOS:

'Traditional' institutions who demand the most highly qualified graduates and are feeder institutions to a 'closed-shop' of businesses and professions 'Enterprise' institutions who understand the challenges that their students will face and are underpinning their curriculum with employability and enterprise to the long-term benefit of their students

EMPLOYERS:

Business leaders who view employability as a one-way street. Universities being expected to deliver suitably equipped graduates without their participation or input

Business leaders who understand the employability agenda. Engaged in the process they offer opportunities for students to develop and, thereby ensure a continuous flow of employable graduates

3.5 UK Characteristics

Competition in the UK higher education market is increasing after the publication and implementation of the 2010 Browne Report. Customer (i.e. potential student) focused marketing and the ability to offer far more than simply an academic qualificationis at the forefront of institutional systems. Inclusion of key employability skills and the ability to offer a complete package sees universities prosper; with more individualised student experiences also increasing.

The transitional process is not likely to be either simplistic or smooth; universities will ultimately need to tackle the changes in orientation which the review suggests. Retaining academic excellence as the primary indicator and driver of reputation, institutions will also need to consider the broader range of services which are provided in order to remain successful. Such challenges can only be met using a two-way dialogue between institutions and customer bases; the needs and expectation of the students should be incorporated into the design and delivery of courses.

There are likely to be an equal or at least significant set of factors which slow this progression. Whilst national government policy and universities at a strategic level are pushing forwards, there has, historically, been a fear of change and a deeply entrenched conservatism to overcome. There are also more pragmatic issues to address in order for the transitional phase to be deemed a success; issues such as student expectation and aspiration. Graduate expectations have often been found to contradict with the world that these students' enter. Sarfraz Manzoor's article in Britain's The *Guardian* (Manzoor, 2010), '*Ready and able*', examined these issues and found well entrenched and unrealistic expectations:

"…with[in] six months she would be in a high-powered job in sound design and really loving it."

"… [I] wanted to do something that was exciting, I am not happy just doing nine to five, I want a way of life not just a job."

"… [I would] not expect to start on anything less than £30,000 a year."

(Source: Manzoor, 2010)

Such expectations highlight the complex issues surrounding student self-awareness, the understanding of the employment market and the level of engagement individuals have historically had with employability skills in the longer term. Educational standards in the UK are demonstrably rising year on year, and so the observed discrepancy is likely to arise from one of four key areas:

1. Graduates are not accustomed to failure, resulting in unrealistic expectations;

2. Graduates are not prepared for the wider competitive market which they are faced with, the challenges they will be presented with or the elements necessary for success;

3. The expectation that opportunities will be available purely on the basis of acquiring a particular academic degree or level of skill;

4. A more general over-confidence in their abilities and the opportunities available.

UK Graduates' somewhat optimistic approach to the current job market and the expectation of individuals is summarised neatly by Will Corder; recruitment advisor for Kimberly-Clark (cited in Manzoor, 2010):

"I find that there are quite a few people who apply to us who can't even spell Kimberly-Clark – even though it is written on the

application form. A lot of people go to university for the sake of it because they think that it is the right thing to do. So that makes a lot of graduates. Universities are still selling the idea to people that if they go to university they are guaranteed a great job at the end of it, and that's just not the case anymore." (Will Corder, Recruitment Advisor, Kimberly-Clark)

3.6 Chinese characteristics

In 1999 the Chinese Government decided to enlarge the scale of higher education enrolment in order to increase the overall quality of the Chinese labour market. Subsequently millions of young people have taken the opportunity to go on to gain a tertiary education and to increase their individual job prospects. In 2003, when these new graduates entered the employment market for the first time, Chinese society experienced a distinct rise in unemployment. Since then the education sector as a whole (government, education institutions, employers and students) has begun to consider the issue of graduate employability as more central to the learning experience.

3.6.1 Barriers to Chinese graduate employability

Prior to the rapid expansion outlined above, China's economic climate was centre-orientated and there was less diversity within the workforce. Central government played a role in the distribution of human resources and also the job market more generally for graduates once they left education. As employment was effectively guaranteed on graduation there were increased levels of passivity and also a lack of ambition and enthusiasm amongst university graduates entering the workforce.

Universities themselves were understandably not wholly sensitive to the needs of either employers or graduates. Institutions often did not recognise the detailed needs of a diverse workplace or the specific requirements of graduates. A large divide existed between the needs of employers, recognition of that need by H.E.I's and the delivery of skills addressing these needs to students. The development of Chinese markets has led to older centralised economic forces being replaced with market-driven strategies.

The associated labour market is also undergoing relatively major changes and the relationships between participants of the market have become increasingly complex.

The Chinese government is no longer solely responsible for the distribution of graduates. The influence exerted on the labour market more generally is also reducing and the focus has started to become more employer led. In keeping with this market-driven strategy, employers now select qualified candidates using criteria designed for that specific role. Alongside this are the increased levels of choice available to graduates, enabling the selection of preferred employment location and type. However the increased levels of intake (and graduate) numbers will have a direct impact on the levels of competition for each post, and issues of employability will rise accordingly.

The continua outlined in the previous sections of this chapter represent a wider framework of integration (from low integration to highly integrated skills); the Chinese situation has some markedly different characteristics to that of the UK and the illustrations can be extended to include the following barrier characteristics.

Chinese government barrier characteristics

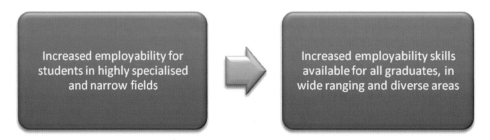

The so-called 'information asymmetry' of the older Chinese labour market to some extent impaired the employability of graduates (Guo, 2009). There had been some difficulties in universities obtaining reliable and timely information from employers and, thus, their courses could not reflect the needs of the workplace accurately. Additionally, such information asymmetry caused universities to provide no formal guidance services to their students; thereby not allowing individuals to alleviate the situation.

Residence regulation compounded these information barriers; new students were required to move their residence registration to that of the place of study and, following graduation, to the place of work. Some commented that this situation represented a distinct barrier; reducing the employability of graduates (Zeng, 2004; Zhang and Zhao, 2007). Primarily the impact of residence registration was on localised economies, there fore, there was little or no incentive to increase the employability of graduates outside of the local area at any given time. Secondly, the residence characteristics limited the centralised funding which could be accessed by those in greatest need of specific and dedicated employability skills funds.

Chinese university barrier characteristics

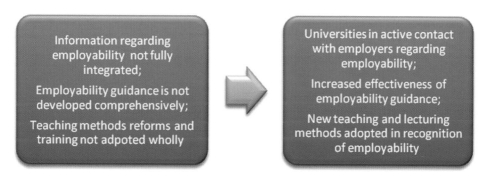

The full integration of employability skills into Chinese universities inherently means the same institutions taking an active role in its delivery,and is central to forming a strong link with employers. Some universities have not made this connection as strong as possible (see Zeng, 2004); and so barriers were created. The requirements of employers in the labour market should be completely integrated in order for students to develop the necessary skills.

The information received by institutions from employers should also form the basis of consistent and flexible guidance for students, both at design and delivery stages (Zhang and Zhao, 2007).This would again reduce the discrepancy between need and availability;the material made available to students has an influence on the outlook and future career development of the individuals, anything inhibiting this delivery impacts greatly on the matching of employers and candidates. Inhibited delivery of guidance can also impact on a graduates' confidence in obtaining relevant employment; something which itself impacts on employability.

The last university centred barrier is that of inflexible and rigid teaching

Implementing Employability

methods, as was highlighted in the UK. Lecturers in Chinese institutions often have a heuristic style and are not overtly open to the developments of individual students (Wu and Luo, 2011). The imparting of technical and subject knowledge is highly developed and greatly valued, however the negation of motivating teaching techniques impacts on the delivery of employability skills. Learners have limited time to engage in an innovative or personalised plan for development, and also staff have limited time to engage in pedagogical theory in their development.

Chinese employer barrier characteristics

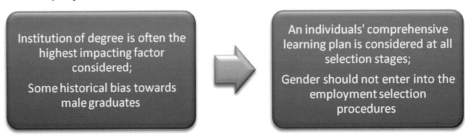

Employment (and employer) bias has become a potential but significant barrier in the modern Chinese market economy. There is, argue Zhang and Zhao (2007), a level of recruitment discrimination in China; two key factors being the institution of award and gender. Historically there was some bias in favour of male graduate recruitment in certain sectors, as well as the expression of favoured institutions; as opposed to the consideration of the whole student package. Such biases clearly alter the level of competition within the sector and create feedback loops; female graduates from less favoured universities experiencing increased employability barriers (Zhang and Zhao, 2007).

Chinese graduate barrier characteristics

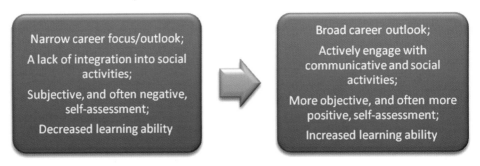

The career choice of many graduates is based solely on location and salary and, whilst these are certainly considerations in terms of employability, there are a far broader range of characteristics to consider. There is a need, argues Zou (2011), for Chinese graduates to have a broader, more flexible approach to seeking post-degree employment.

The ability to communicate effectively has been identified in previous sections as an important skill to developing employability. Under the single-child policy in China a large proportion of families have an only child and so the need to engage in social and communicative skills development is key (Guo, 2009). The often poor communication ability of some Chinese graduates severely limits their competitiveness in the workplace.

The family unit has an extraordinarily large impact on Chinese graduates' career planning. A large proportion of graduates depend entirely on their parents to make key decisions regarding their career development. However the ability of the individuals' parents to make objective, realistic decisions (which are not overestimated or unachievable) has been called into question. Naturally parents make positive claims about their offspring, though in terms of employability it is often a more evidence based approach which is of value. If individuals are not able to fulfil the criteria they have been set by close family members then this will have an impact on their wider employability (Zhang and Zhao, 2007).

Lastly, the ability of an individual to acquire new knowledge and apply it critically and robustly is central to most employers' search to fill vacancies. This learning ability should be a particular focus in graduates (Zou, 2011). The teaching (and learning) styles in Chinese universities are often passive; therefore the development of more critical and active students has been limited.

The 'iron rice bowl' and organisational inertia

Complicating all of the specific factors discussed in the previous sections are deeper economic and cultural factors which serve to cross-cut those influenced by graduates, employers and institutional planning. A system derived largely from previous communist mentalities, the 'iron rice bowl' embodied the notion of a job for life; an individual would be secure in employment for the duration of their lives (Ding et al., 2000). Arguably the notions inherent in such dependency on a single company are deep-rooted within institutional strategies and linked to slow human resource changes. This organisational inertia creates a slower market for graduates to enter as well as decreasing the importance of employability skills integration.

Although the concept of a job for life created and maintained by the state (as well as such employment being guaranteed) has been largely phased out with increased competition amongst the manufacturing sector (Ding et al., 2000), the lasting effects potentially impact on all sectors. There is a great deal of organisational inertia and the changes have been slow in taking effect, thus the hypothesised argument is that conceptions of complete (and guaranteed) employment in specific sectors for life not only affect the institutional attitudes of strategy formers but also students, lecturing staff and employers. Such attitudes are, clearly, hard to break with.

The model outlined in section 3.2 proposed that it is creativity, and the embedding of such creativity within the lecturing staff, which addresses most of these factors. However, this fostered culture amongst staff has to be integrated at every level, including the culture more widely. Certainly, in the present case, some of the barriers discussed would be significantly reduced if clear communicative skills and dynamism were core values of the H.E teaching process (Sweeney et al., 2009).

3.6.2 Tentative solutions proposed

The specific nature of the limitations in integrating employability in Chinese universities is addressed in the following sections, however these are micro-level observations and fall within the scope of the broader model outlined in section 3.2. Whilst strategic, employer and institutional change are fundamental in addressing these issues; it is the fostering of creativity at the point of delivery which is central. In the three main areas discussed there have been significant moves towards removing (or at least limiting) the effects on employment prospects. Strategies developed for addressing these inhibiting factors are clearly relevant and are also applicable more broadly.

Governmental change

The strong links between society, government and education in China mean that employability issues are at the forefront of policy development. In order for these relationships to be strengthened and further developed the transfer of information between institutions and other organisations needs to be as smooth as possible, alongside well developed communication pathways and strong links between the market as a whole and students. Better information to universities will clearly increase the effectiveness of any integration.

Secondly, changes addressing the labour market should be implemented by the government. Constraints which are not the fault of the student or the employer, and could not be removed by better educational or transitional policies, could effectively be addressed by the state. Reducing the impact of residency and other inhibiting factors would significantly increase the employability of a large number of individuals without the need for wholesale strategic change. Lastly, the implementation of professional training would certainly impact greatly on the barriers mentioned in the preceding sections (Guo, 2009). The integration of skills development, linked directly to employment, would also cross-cut a number of other factors.

University change

Whilst broader change is important, it is within an institutional setting where more direct measures can be employed; the role of the university is fundamental in addressing employability skills integration in China. Inclusion of material from employers into core and specialised modules for skills development has been crucial to employability in other areas, and something historically which has not happened in China (Wu and Luo, 2011). The curriculum design, across a wide range of courses, would benefit from input and flexible arrangements by key sector professionals.

Increasing diversity in the graduate cohorts could also be reflected in course material and delivery; the separation of research focused and practitioner orientated institutions would represent a progression towards a more integrated approach. Such a diversification would certainly impact on the responsibilities of the graduates themselves; though increased specificity of employability skills would make each individual more competitive in the marketplace.

Universities are central to guiding individuals through their academic career in terms of information for future career planning (Wu and Luo, 2011; Zou, 2011). The criticism that students are often overly subjective about their self-assessment could be tackled by increased uptake of career services; the ability to choose a suitable position within a competitive market. The availability of market information, the size of competition and their relative strengths would clearly enable individual graduates to approach employers in a more comprehensive manner.

The more traditional teaching methods of the Chinese education system, whilst strong in information transition,potentially limit students' innovative and critical abilities (Wu and Luo, 2011). Indeed a firm suggestion has been put to the institutions in the form of a three stage plan:

1. An incentive mechanism to improve the motivation for innovative teaching mechanisms in Chinese universities.

2. An incentive mechanism to encourage breadth of teaching methods on single modules.

3. A training programme which encompasses the above into continuing development for staff.

Alongside the development of staff and teaching methods, Chinese institutions would also benefit from the inclusion of *work-based learning* modules. According to one key survey, the majority of Chinese graduates had undertaken little or no practice based learning during their qualification (MyCOS survey, Luo et al., 2011). Such curriculum amendments would increase the employability of graduates greatly. Lastly, there have been calls for Chinese institutions to do more for graduates in the time after graduation; to provide a network of alumni and on-going support for career planning and development.

Student attitudinal change

Arguably the most dominant factor in the employability of university graduates is the attitudinal beliefs of the learners themselves. The career outlook of the individuals must match both the labour market and a realistic self-assessment. If a student (or their parents) considers a sector of employment to be 'cold' then the traditional motivation was to stay at home until a 'hot' job was offered (Zuo, 2011). This clearly creates a situation whereby certain employment types are over-subscribed and others heavily under-recruited.

A large number of students receive almost identical training and development with little specificity for employability, and the majority suffer low employability as a result. A more specified career outlook would enable students to develop comprehensive and applicable abilities. This is coupled with the need to disassociate the career prospects of the individual from their parents' wishes. Whilst parental involvement is clearly central, a move towards student-led choice may prove beneficial. This would increase the objectivity of self-assessment and give individuals a more realistic view of their place within a rapidly changing workplace. Overall, individuals should increasingly recognise the specificity of employability within the market–driven workplace in China today. A moderate move away from parental choice and towards geographic and societal mobility would greatly increase the employability prospects for the majority of learners.

Less practically, it has also been argued that Chinese students should increase their levels of communicative and social abilities. Extra-curricular and post-graduation activities, in collaboration with other student bodies, are central to producing well rounded, employable, graduates (Guo, 2009).  The integration of more group-based learning into degree courses would certainly aid the process, as would the increase of levels of social activities such as clubs.

3.7 Summary

This chapter has outlined the integration of employability skills throughout the learning process. A multitude of techniques for em-bedding employability across the whole syllabus (for a wide range of differing students) were outlined and the notion of increasing the levels of both specificity and integration with level of qualification was introduced. Overall a number of recommendations were made to enhance the labour market effectiveness of graduates through a model of integration.

However, the integrative process is by no means simple and a wide range of barriers were considered. These largely fell into consistent themes around the learners, teaching and the strategic management of educational facilities (at both local and national levels). These problems were subsequently outlined in both a UK and Chinese context. In the UK, increased competition leads to a need for more diversification in employability and student led change. Whilst similar in China there is a wide need for culture change at an individual and national level to integrate both social and communicative skills. The uniqueness of the Chinese market development in the last 10 years has also posed key challenges for the integration of employability skills.

Ideally the skills associated with employability would be of equal importance to learners, employers, lecturing staff and national policy makers. These skills would enhance a diverse range of graduate skills which match the needs of market-driven workplace competition. Graduates could make independent choices based on local and national conditions to best match the current employment situation. Clearly, these conditions are often unmet for a number of reasons and so this chapter has highlighted the need to balance all of these tensions to best aid graduates in far from ideal circumstances.

SUM-UP
- ✓ Employability should be embedded across the curriculum as well as incorporated into extra-curricular activities.
- ✓ There are significant barriers to integrating employability skills.
- ✓ These barriers exhibit striking similarities and differences between Chinese and UK education systems.

4 Student Centred Approaches to Employability

With applications for every degree course place standing at an all-time high, the need for positive outcomes by both students and their parents heightens the focus on employability. With increasing numbers of students graduating every year employers have more choice, and so graduates today must stand out. When looking for candidates to join their organisations, a degree or other qualification is simply a starting point; employers then want to see what else candidates have to offer. Too often students believe that their degree is the passport to success; that universities will guide them through the employment minefield. This chapter examines what strategies can be employed by students themselves to increase their employability.

4.1 Student roles

Many universities are striving to support and equip their students; however a student cannot be a passive member of his or her own employability development. Investing substantially in the development of employability programs, whatever a university puts in place, is irrelevant if the individual student does not have the motivation to develop their own skill set whilst studying. Learners' 'life-wide' experiences are central to forming and developing highly employable graduates (Jackson, 2011).

Dr Glen Crust, of the Teaching & Learning Directorate (Careers & Employability), Plymouth University, has identified four clear roles that students take on within the Higher Education setting.

1. **Customers:** buying the educational services that Universities provide, focusing on the value individual courses provide and the benefits faculties offer, students will become more discerning customers with the impending increases in tuition fees.

2. **Raw Material:** each student is part of the learning experience, the central aspect of the educational process and the element that all universities must be able to attract in order to survive under changing

funding regimes. Universities, whose success is predicated on the quality of the students they can attract and the satisfaction levels they provide, will be required to compete more vigorously for quality students.

3. **Product:** each student is the output of the educational process; at the end of their studies each being a more rounded, accomplished and employable individual.

4. **Shop-floor workers:** students are involved day-to-day in the production process. Their engagement with their studies lies at the heart of their successful completion and will ultimately shape their future direction.

Educational and employability outcomes are ultimately driven by the complex interplay between these four roles. To achieve the results that both the university and the student desire, course managers must appreciate the multiple facets of the student experience in order to draw them together and produce the employable graduates of the future. Education is a service and as such the relationship between the provider (lecturer, university) and the consumer (student, cohort) cannot be ignored. The influence of the lecturer to inspire, and of the design of the course to equip the students with the tools to face the challenges of working life, are inextricably linked with the consumers; their involvement is critical, they are directly involved in this production process. Their relationship with the lecturer and their engagement in the process ultimately affects the quality of the end product; their employability.

Such relationships (between the service provider and the consumers of this service) reflect the growing school of thought around the *'co-production'* in the provision of public services. Co-production recognises that service providers and service users cannot work in isolation, they need each other and the contribution that each makes in the service provision. This chapter is dedicated to how students can apply tactics and strategies to improve their own employability, giving an overview of some of the ways of adding value to their university experience.

Marc Lintern, Head of Employability at Plymouth University, has identified ten different actions that students can consider in both the UK and China when attempting to enhance their employability. These are presented in the document *'Top Tips for Career Success'* and have been amended and adapted for this chapter. Plymouth University offers a range of opportunities to extend each student's personal and academic development; by taking up these opportunities, the university believes that its graduates will become more employable. Work experience, participation in clubs and societies, voluntary work, choice of dissertation and being a course representative are all things that can add value to a CV and help make a student stand out from their peers.

4.2 Get a part time/vacation job

The Confederation of British Industry (CBI), in their Education and Skills Survey 2010, clearly identified the importance of work experience for new graduates. 88% of employers believe that work experience is vital for young people before leaving school or college. With no influence over the state of the labour market that they face on gradua-tion, students must equip themselves  to cope with whatever conditions they will face (CBI, 2010). Johnson and Burden (2003) identified the fact that many of the skills required of graduates could only be learned in 'real life' situations. Irrespective of the efforts made by HEIs to simulate work scenarios there is only a limited extent to which they can successfully 'teach' these skills and attributes.

Studies suggest that it is not simply the formal curriculum elements, but the whole environment that contributes to students' learning (Pascarella and Terenzini, 1991; Astin, 1997). Little et al., (2006) identified that for many students work-based learning does not take place in the formal setting of placements or other university led activities, but through the jobs that students undertake to finance themselves through higher education. Work experience in any field is important to the majority of employers, suggesting that any type of employment is seen to enhance the development of transferable skills that employers are looking for. Whilst such employment may not be directly relevant to the student's area of study or future career path, the benefits accrue not necessarily from the experience of work itself but from the learning derived from the experience and from reflecting upon it (Little et al., 2006).

At Plymouth University it has been identified that securing paid employment, be it part-time or across vacation periods, is invaluable and has strong pedagogic support in enhancing future employment opportunities. Securing these types of employment clearly benefits students in a number of ways in both the long and short terms:

- Earning extra money can support the student experience, instilling greater personal financial awareness and management skills;

- Gives students the key work experience and associated transferable skills which can increase future employability;

- Allows students to 'road test' possible future jobs and work environments, allowing them to make more considered employment choices upon graduation;

- All employment allows students to develop, build and expand CVs which are more attractive to potential employers who are increasingly demanding of their recruits;

- Employment develops students' networking skills. Understanding how to develop effective business relationships and create effective working relationships with colleagues;

- Some employment may offer opportunities for summer overseas travel where students can gain invaluable experience of international working practices. The understanding of divergent cultural and working norms being an increasingly valuable tool for graduates in a globalised economy; and

- Most employers will not consider people without work experience. Any type of employment will enhance the development of sought after transferable skills.

(Source: Plymouth University, 2011)

4.3 Volunteer

In the face of a recovering economy which is struggling to emerge from the recession in the UK, both the public and private sectors are tightening their belts, thereby reducing the number and quality of opportunities open to students to secure ad-hoc work experience. An alternative is offered through volunteering. Offering many of the opportunities that students can gain from paid employment, volunteering reflects positively on an individual's commitment.

In the UK, the development of the "Big Society" by the coalition government to "drive and empower communities" (BBC, 2010) was argued to open up a wealth of opportunity for individuals to get involved in areas of their passion and to make a difference to society as a whole. For students, engaging with the volunteering opportunities potentially on offer to them would boost their employability credentials for a number of reasons:

- Engagement in volunteering would enhance student studies in both formal (if working in an area associated with their academic course) and generic (through their participation in a 'work' situation) employability skills;

- Due to the nature of the volunteering process students may benefit from access to free training courses and gain qualifications and accreditation which support the volunteer offering process;

- Students will learn new skills which are embedded more deeply by being involved in an environment that is the perfect fit with their own interests;

- Volunteering shows a strong commitment to a career that interests the student and that they would want to pursue; a would-be photographer may want to volunteer to work on a local newspaper. Such unpaid 'placements' have traditionally been required of people looking to gain employment in socalled glamorous industries such as the media. With increasing graduate numbers and a shrinking pool of opportunities more and more graduates are looking at this method as a way of getting a foot in the employment door;

- There are some sectors where voluntary experience is essential when applying for jobs;

- Students not only gain valuable experience but benefit from the feel good factor. Meeting new people, working in new and challenging environments means students not only have the opportunity to give something back but also to have fun in the process;

- There is the chance for students to step away from the norms and do something completely different and challenging. Such experiences are engaging for employers, offering a potential foot in the door and instilling a wider, more rounded perspective frequently missing in potential graduate recruits.

Volunteering activities are only limited by the scope of the student's imagination. The breadth and commitment in volunteering can be dictated by the student; from once a term, every month or an hour a week. The value in terms of employability is unquestioned, with 73% of employers selecting candidates who have volunteering experience.

4.4 Do a work placement

"If we recruited on the basis of degree level, we'd just use a computer but we're looking for examples of leadership, teamwork and commercial awareness which are usually found in extracurricular activities and work experience. In short your degree alone won't get you a job. You need work experience too". Tim Forster, Head of Resourcing Media, Pricewaterhouse Coopers

The value of work experience to students in developing their future employability is without question. Students who have had real experience come out on top in all employment stakes. Working in 1999, Bowes and Harvey (cited in Little et al., 2006) found that 70% of students who had undertaken work experience were in full time employment, compared to 55% of those students who had not gained experience within the labour market. These toe-holds into employment were seen to be of particular benefit to graduates in the early stages of their careers.

The CBI/EDI Education and Skills Survey 2010 found that 56% of employers saw work experience as the biggest single contributing factor in preparing young people for the world they face.

> *"… we look for graduates who can bring more to the table than pure academic achievement. Typically, the graduates that shine have work or life experience which differentiates them from other applicants".* (Gaynor Sykes, Graduate Resourcing Manager, Vodafone UK)

Previous exposure to the workplace is viewed as indispensable by many businesses; and business *must* play an active part in the delivery of providing high quality work experience. Knight and Yorke (2004) identified that work experience in any setting is an important consideration for employers when recruiting. Formal work-based learning in a business environment enhances students' learning experiences whilst providing them with the opportunity to acquire and hone work-related skills. The CBI identified a three-way partnership involving employers, students and universities (Figure 4.1), to create placements that ultimately add value for the students.

The nature of placements may vary. It may be that they are a compulsory precursor to professional practice after graduation as is the case in teaching, or alternatively they may offer students the opportunity to gain commercial experience in placements that can last as little as two weeks, or for as long as a year.

The CBI sees the benefits derived from placements for individual students as numerous:

- Placement (of whatever form) gives a context to students about the true nature of employment. Students are required to use the theories that they have studied and apply them in real situations. It also improves academic performance and provides ideas for final year projects, providing a 'taster' of a future career;

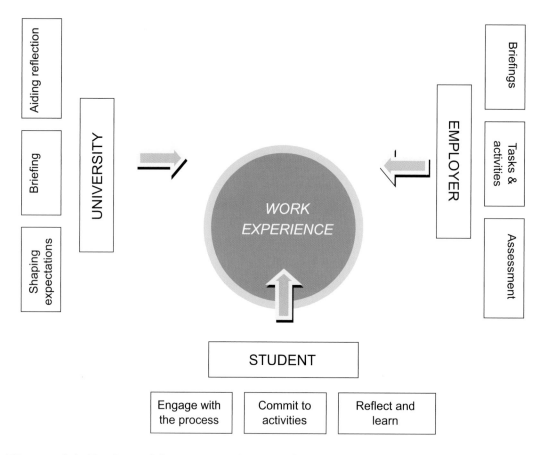

Figure 4.1 Partnership approach to embedding employability through work experience

(Source: Adapted from CBI, 2010)

- Networking is pivotal to career progression. Work placements offer students the opportunity to start along this road, making new friends and more importantly developing an important contact book which can potentially boost them up the employment ladder - up to 60% of job vacancies are not advertised but filled internally or through external networking;

- The majority of placements are paid. In times of austerity, for placements with small companies or in industries where competition is high (e.g. media organisations) students must be prepared to consider unpaid placements. Universities are eager not to encourage this but it is increasingly the norm that placement offices face, particularly in the public sector. University, employer and student must be clear that the value of the placement if unpaid is significant enough to justify this. If a student is offered in-kind benefits: in-house training, opportunities to attend major conferences and support, offers such as these are invaluable;

- Ultimately a placement will add real, practical business experience to the student's CV. With a degree being no longer an effective tool for differentiation, employers look for direct and applicable experience when screening candidates. If that experience can be reinforced by having a placement employer as a reference, prospective employers will gain a real insight into a student's potential to do the job, thereby reducing the risk to the employer;

- For many employers a placement is part of their recruitment process and students may find themselves with the offer of final year sponsorship or the offer of a job upon the successful completion of their studies. Through the formal approach of placement interviews, employers have already researched the market and been able to identify the students they believe best fit their organisation. Employers can then assess the qualities of their placement students at relatively low risk and can identify those students who they may want to establish a longer term relationship with. Businesses are increasingly looking to foster longer term relationships with universities or specific faculties giving them a 'first look' at the emerging talent and offering students the best opportunity to get the choice of the placements on offer; and

- A placement is potentially financially rewarding for students, and it does provide the foundations of networks. A placement also builds students' confidence, self-discipline and sense of responsibility. These interpersonal skills help shape students into 'rounded' young people who are best equipped to cope with whatever conditions they face (CBI, 2010).

4.5 Plan your personal development

Increasing numbers of universities identify the need to provide dedicated resources designed to support student employability. This is not simply limited to the revision of pedagogic methods designed to support employability, but an emphasis on business/industry engagement or the development of effective teaching strategies. Many universities are developing the use of students' Personal Development Plans (PDP), which provide students with a framework for self-analysis, identify any gaps that may exist in their skills and offer opportunities to acquire those skills (CBI, 2009).

An example of an online PDP is 'PebblePad', the system currently used across Plymouth University. PebblePad is a way to get students to focus on these issues by requiring them to consider their own development needs. The system allows those students who engage with it to make a start on collating evidence about their skills, competencies, attitudes and attributes from their academic and extra-curricular lives. It also provides a number of tangible benefits which can help students focus on their longer term career development:

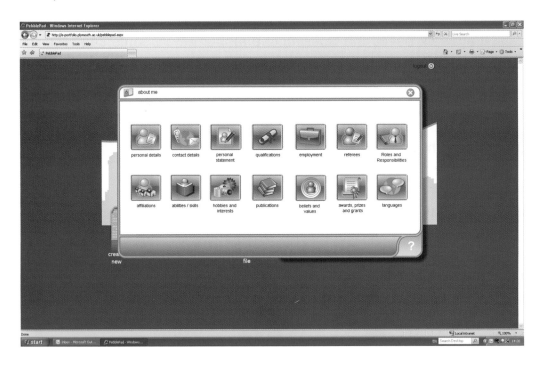

Fig 4.2 PebblePad @ University of Plymouth

- Every individual student can store all the evidence of their achievements, be it academic, clubs and organisations, work placements, volunteering or ad-hoc work in one secure and password protected digital vault;

- Students can use the software to create any number of presentation portfolios and CVs, based on the information and evidence that they upload onto the system;

- Students can use the range of tools in PebblePad (Fig 4.2 above), to help them reflect on their achievements, set out their career and personal goals and aspirations and to share them with their tutor, peers or anyone else they choose;

- Each PebblePad account is accessible from anywhere in the world at any time. To meet the changing demands of the ways in which students access information and data PebblePad can also be accessed from mobile devices such as PDA's, mobile phones and tablets; and

- The assets that students develop in PebblePad are not lost the day they walk out of the door for the last time. Students can take their assets with them when they graduate and either migrate them to a new free PebblePad account or start off a new PDP program using the materials that they have spent time developing.

PDP tools such as PebblePad are invaluable to students, increasing their confidence and showing them how they learn and in what settings they thrive. However, as discussed previously, students cannot remove themselves from these development opportunities and are not passive bystanders. Andrews and Higson (2008) identified the tendency by which students are viewed as universalistic, rational investors in education who view the labour market in a uniform and stereotypical way (Rees et al., 1997). Such a view negates the different orientations and work-related identities that students develop in relation to their own future employability. The provision of, and support for, PDP across institutions allows students to add value and context to their educational qualifications, which are no longer the basis of recruitment decisions, making them stand out from other candidates, all of whom possess similar credentials (Andrews and Higson, 2008).

4.6 Plug your skill gaps

Employers are dissatisfied with the level of skill shown by graduates leaving university: 24% are dissatisfied with graduates' problem-solving skills and 26% with their self-management skills (CBI, 2010). The Education and Skills survey further identifies 39% of businesses who feel that graduates should have greater work experience and 46% expressing dissatisfaction with graduates' business and customer awareness.

Whilst HEIs can (and are) taking steps to address the latter concerns it is incumbent on students to identify those gaps within their skill set and to take steps to address them. Only a small minority of graduates directly use their degree disciplines as the basis for their subsequent employment (Baker and Henson, 2010), and so rely largely on their degree course to supply them with the skills that will allow them to compete effectively in the job market. Wickramasinghe and Perera (2010) draw out the two aspects of these broader employability skills:

1. **Subject skills:** Students usually leave with a good appreciation of their chosen subject area. This is often not relevant to their ultimate career path and no longer sufficient in meeting what prospective employers are looking for; and

2. **Transferable skills:** The personal abilities that an individual student takes from one role to another used within any profession at any stage within their career. It is these skills that students need to analyse to determine if they possess them to the required standard and, if not, take the necessary steps to enhance these skills to become more employable.

Atkins (1999) suggests that there is no reason for employers to have common skills requirements; they will naturally vary by region, industry and business size. The skills required to succeed in marketing, HR and finance roles (as will be discussed in the results chapters; 7, 8 and 9) are different. Marketers in the media may, for example, require a differently nuanced skills set to marketers employed in blue-chip FMCG organisations. The skills required in different geographies are under-researched, with the majority of studies being limited to Western countries (Wickramasinghe and Perera, 2010). The subsequent comparative analysis in this book, of China and the UK, will therefore offer students clear guidance on the skills that are expected in each country.

The difference between a future employer's and a graduate's perception regarding skills requirements may differ significantly (Zhiwen and van der Heijden, 2008).By understanding and engaging with their own employability, students can determine what the employment market is looking for and identify any shortcomings. The use of PDP tools and techniques (as outlined previously) is part of the solution for students who are ultimately looking to recognise and plug these skills gaps.

To address such gaps, students must undertake objective self-analysis. A realistic skills audit will identify shortcomings and focus students' minds on aspects that, when successfully developed, will improve job prospects. However many students may be unwilling or unable to undertake such a review. Ill-equipped to assess the challenges of the working environment, and with unrealistic expectations of their relative position within the job market, such students will be disadvantaged in their search for graduate employment.

The CBI (2010) identifies 10% of employers who are concerned with graduates' basic skills (14% with literacy/use of English and 9% with numeracy). Clearly the first step that students should take is to strengthen these skills. With 24% doubting graduates problem-solving skills, the next step to ensure success in the employment market is to learn essential skills in critical thinking, analysis and evaluation as well as in communicating and presenting ideas effectively.

Forward-looking students must also engage and understand emerging business issues and philosophies. Business ethics, sustainability, the triple bottom line and corporate social responsibility are examples of areas of increasing importance and profile across business. Whilst universities are engaging with these rapidly developing issues, the very nature of the academic process lags behind the developments that are happening on the ground. Those students that proactively engage with the contemporary issues facing business, and can offer informed opinions, will enhance the opportunities open to them.

4.7 Add to your qualifications

The notion that a degree is a "passport to employment" has been relegated to the past (Harvey cited in Baker and Henson, 2010). The value of a degree is great. Graduates earn around 50% more than non-graduates and as a group enjoy double the number of job promotions (DfES, 2003). However the changing notion of graduate skills and competencies (Tomlinson, 2008), and the oversupply of graduates has resulted in a decline in the status and value of a degree qualification. Whilst a degree no longer offers the same levels of differential advantage in the market place, employers do assign it value in terms of the ability to undertake work-based learning, the development of inter-personal skills and as the best indicator of mental ability (Yorke and Knight, 2007).

Faced with ever increasing competition for graduate employment, one way for students to stand out from the crowd is by adding to their qualifications. A postgraduate qualification significantly increases the chances of finding meaningful employment within the first six months of graduation. Universities have traditionally focused on the delivery of such traditional academic qualifications (masters and doctoral), whilst beneficial in many ways these qualifications are not the sole route that graduates may wish to follow. Increasingly business is demanding vocational and professional qualifications that reflect the demands of the modern economy. In business related disciplines, neither degrees nor postgraduate qualification content should address only issues of direct academic significance.

The value of recognised industry qualifications, such as the CPD structure offered in the UK by the Chartered Institute of Marketing, should not be overlooked by students and program directors. By identifying what businesses are looking for in its recruits, and developing a mixed economy approach towards the qualifications package they offer (see Chapter10; MSc Marketing Management and Strategy, Plymouth University), students will enhance their C.V.s with a more compelling offer for prospective employers.

4.8 Get a mentor

There is more that businesses can do to support students beyond the provision of placements. One in five employers (21%, CBI, 2010) identified that the most important thing that a business can do is to encourage their employees to act as student mentors.

The Chartered Institute of Personnel and Development (CIPD, 2011) defines mentoring as "a technique for allowing the transmission of knowledge, skills and experience in a supportive and challenging environment." The skills used in successful mentoring are much like those employed in effective business coaching; questioning, listening, clarifying, reframing and many of the same models are used.Mentoring is now widely seen as being of great value, particularly to students who may face some kind of disadvantage;offering students a sympathetic individual with whom they can confidently address issues around disability and disclosure.

"I have gained many life skills from taking part in the Mentoring Programme"

By building positive relationships, mentoring establishes common ground and a sense of shared experience between students and their mentors. The real power in mentoring, however, is that it helps students build an informed vision of what their future may hold (CBI, 2010).

This type of supportive relationship with an experienced industry professional is of value to individuals at all stages of their careers. Mentoring relationships can be long term or short term; working as a way of inducting employees, as a form of staff development across departments and as a means of simple skills transfer. Irrespective of the duration, an effective mentoring relationship is a learning opportunity for both parties (CIPD, 2011). For graduates who are just entering the job market, the considered advice of a mentor is invaluable. An effective mentor should be part coach, part project manager; guiding students around some of the pitfalls that may face them.

By challenging students, mentors give clarity to careers ideas as they increase understanding of job roles. Their experience helps instruct students how they may enter a particular industry and suggest strategies that they can employ to set and achieve these goals. A mentor's experience is invaluable to graduates and the insight that they can bring influences the way students make a first impression in the job market through the development of effective C.Vs. A strong, supportive mentoring relationship for a student will build their self-confidence, enabling them to feel more self-assured about starting a graduate job.

4.9 Join clubs and societies or become a course rep or Students' Union officer

Whilst opportunities to enhance students' employability can be found in the courses developed around learning outcomes, placements and ad-hoc work experience, the value of any complimentary experience offered through the academic process remains. Joining clubs and societies, representing courses on academic panels or running for Students' Union officer are all effective methods of developing valuable employability skills.

The willingness to participate and to give up spare time to engage in activities that benefit others reflects an engagement in personal development, and also reflects positively with potential future employers. Whilst potentially informal, the experiences gained certainly enhance a student's C.V; by taking on official or quasi-official roles students develop their leadership, coaching, management and organisational skills.

Additionally, there are often opportunities for students to become engaged in CPD; be it in the shape of attending training courses or gaining practical qualifications that support such roles, developing skills in negotiation, learning how to manage time and meetings effectively or to become active listeners and accomplished presenters of their fellow students' views, individuals who are proactive in taking on such positions become better placed to succeed in the job market.

4.10 Meet employers

As highlighted in the previous discussion around the values of placement experience, meeting and engaging with potential employers adds significant value to the student job-hunter. The development of dialogue with employers through recruitment fairs or participation in curricular events (for example the Flux Business game) offers some insight into the demands of business and the expectations of employers. An understanding of what an organisation is really looking for in an employee is invaluable intelligence for a student looking to improve their competitive advantage in the employment market.

Stephen Covey in his '*Seven Habits of Highly Effective People*' outlined the value of being proactive, and showed that those students who understood their aims and developed strategies to deliver them equipped themselves far better (Covey, 2004). By engaging with employers, students will find out which organisations are recruiting, how active that process is; the roles they may be looking to fill and expectations of the skills, experience and capabilities expected of candidates.

Developing these relationships may further allow students to ask their own specific questions about the organisation, thereby getting a real feel for what an organisation might be like to work for, exactly what the role might include and how they might make themselves stand out at interview. The prospect of engaging with employers will be daunting for many students, however those that can "begin with the end in mind" (Covey, 2004) will ultimately equip themselves better to succeed.

4.11 Get some careers advice

For the role of employability to gain credibility within academic circles, it needs to involve academics and senior management alongside careers advisors (Baker and Henson, 2010). Careers advisors are an invaluable resource for students who, if properly utilised, will help shape their future success. Academic staff members often have limited experience of business life and therefore their experiences are limited regarding what businesses are really looking for (Zhiwen and van der Heijden, 2008), careers advisors provide a bridge into the world of employment.

"I think a proactive careers service is a really good idea because I found in my first year holiday that all my friends would be disappearing off on placements, whilst I was unaware of what opportunities were available. I had no clue that these things even existed. If someone had

flagged this up at the beginning of my first year, that would have been really helpful." (Graduate working at Innocent Drinks, quoted CBI, 2010)

Many students using the Careers Service have no idea what they are going to do in the future. Tomlinson (2008) identified the subjective nature of employability and the relationship between how students perceive the labour market and their types of disposition towards their future employability (see figure 4.3, overleaf).

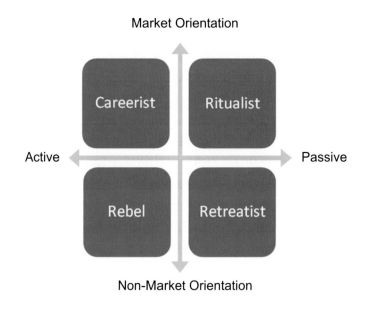

Figure 4.3   Student employability orientation

(Source: adapted from Tomlinson, 2008)

The challenge for careers advisors is how to inform the students' understanding of the labour market. Those students who recognise the important insight into the expectations of employers that university careers advisors offer have increased focus on their future employment direction. Taking careers advice early can help identify the options that are available. Practical skills can also be honed by giving training, guidance and support in the development of C.V.s, and how to complete applications effectively. Students' Unions also offer a range of activities designed to help students apply for jobs. The skills that are supported are not the same as employability skills but are designed to help students, for example by providing evidence to demonstrate a competency (CBI, 2009). The extra-curricular activities that are offered help students identify their skills gaps and offer them a means to fill them through training.

SUM-UP

- ✓ Universities have a responsibility to support employability, work readiness and mobility in their graduates.
- ✓ Universities must equip students with the two aspects of employability skills: subject skills and transferable skills.
- ✓ Business demands more rounded graduates and requires graduates to have the skills and experience to make an impact.

5 Culture, Learning and Employability

The impact of culture on the learning environment is profound. Alongside the discipline specifics mentioned in previous chapters it is impossible to conceptualise integration of employability into learning materials without a consideration of cultural factors. Broad and extremely complex, culture impacts upon almost all aspects of a student's life. Culture shapes students' learning environments and the skills and knowledge base that they develop through all stages in their educational development. Definitions of culture vary and even in 1952 over 160 definitions were identified in the literature (Kroeder and Kluckholn, 1952).Common to most definitions are themes of similarity of thought, feeling and acting which are all sourced from common values, ideas and notions within society (Wallace, 1970; Cushman and King, 1985; Schudson, 1994; Jusdanis, 1995). Incorporating elements of many of these, a workable definition might be:

> *Culture is the total way of life in a society; it is the collective programming of the mind which distinguishes the members of human groups from another in terms of shared beliefs, the ideologies, and the norms that influence the organisational action taking.* (Adapted from: Hofstede, 1984)

5.1 Cultural distance between China and the West

> *"Psychic distance refers to a measure of how far a country is perceived to be away from another in terms of cultural elements like belief systems, language barriers, different attitudes to business, material standards and patterns of behaviour."* (Fletcher and Bohn, 1998).

Cultural difference arguably underpins a great deal of the difference between students and learning material. It is not merely objective traits which form the basis of national and cultural pride but more subjective, ascribed behaviours observed by both insiders and outsiders. Cultural units can range from the clearly defined (i.e. language), through to the more subtle indicators of membership of sub-groups (i.e. beard length/dress). Before a consideration of differing learning styles (and temployability) between Western and Chinese students is provided, it is beneficial to outline more generic measures of cultural difference.

One of these measures is the psychic difference ratings of countries, as defined through the work of Fletcher and Bohn (1998) (based on the work of Hofstede and Bond (1988) and Hofstede (1984; 1994)). This index details the differences exhibited by countries as measured from Australia. Of those examined, China was second most different only to Panama (see table 5.1). Conversely, the UK exhibited similarity second only to the USA. Therefore, there are significant cultural differences between the UK and China and moreover these differences are to be found not only in the objective measures but in more subtle indicators – relevant in this instance are the differences in learning styles.

Table 5.1 Psychic distance rating of countries from Australia

United States	0.1	Sweden	8.8	Mexico	17.6
Great Britain	**0.6**	Argentina	9.2	Greece	18.0
Canada	0.6	Iran	9.3	Indonesia	18.3
New Zealand	0.7	India	9.7	Singapore	19.3
Switzerland	1.5	Kenya	12.2	Korea	20.3
Germany	1.7	Zimbabwe	12.2	Taiwan	20.4
Ireland	1.7	Tanzania	12.2	Hong Kong	20.5
South Africa	2.0	Rwanda	12.2	Chile	20.7
Italy	2.2	Brazil	12.3	Portugal	21.9
Finland	4.7	Turkey	13.6	Yugoslavia	21.9
Netherlands	5.5	Japan	15.2	Peru	23.3
Belgium	6.1	Philippines	15.7	Colombia	23.5
France	6.1	Russia	16.0	Malaysia	23.6
Austria	6.3	Nigeria	16.3	Costa Rica	25.0
Israel	7.1	Ghana	16.3	Venezuela	26.2
Denmark	7.3	Uruguay	16.4	Ecuador	27.4
Norway	7.4	Thailand	16.5	**China**	**29.2**
Spain	8.6	Pakistan	17.3	Panama	31.4

(Source: adapted from Fletcher and Bohn, 1998)

5.2 Differences between Chinese and Western Students

A range of authors have aimed to examine the specific differences between Western and Chinese students, as well as the underlying processes. The collectivist ideals of Chinese society have a great impact on teaching and learning styles, with more frequent large-group teaching and fewer one-to-one sessions (Xiao and Dyson, 1999). Additionally, the presence of a clearly defined hierarchy between teaching staff and students inherently implies a teacher-led process. The role of Confucianism is clear in these teacher-centred learning environments - with modesty of behaviour reducing the level of questioning of the teacher (Chan, 1999). Other values associated with this tradition include:

- Valuing theoretical education more highly than vocational education;
- Viewing learning as a moral duty;
- Hard work and effort are valued more highly than ability;
- Respect for a teacher, and seeing him/her as a model of morality and knowledge (Biggs, 1996; Lee, 1996).

More entrenched differences between Chinese and Western students were noted by Entwistle and Tait, (1994) who found that Chinese students placed emphasis more on memorisation, not as rote learning but as part of a deeper learning process. From a very early age there is a strong emphasis on memory skills and practice through repetition (Cortazzi and Jin, 1996). The impact that this cultural influence has is significant; Chinese students overwhelmingly perform better in subjects related to science and maths skills when compared to western students (Salili, 1996). Whilst clearly a positive impact these differences have led some to argue that Chinese students are less "known for their creativity and original thinking" (Salili, 1996:100); differences which will be expanded in later sections. Despite these relevant findings there is limited direct research examining the differences between Western and Chinese university students.

5.2.1 Learning styles

Cultural difference is by no means the only significant and impacting factor on the way that students learn material and perform in educational activities. Indeed the ancient Greeks recognised that *all* students have differing approaches to learning (Wratcher et al., 1997; Diaz and Cartnal, 1999). These various approaches to the acquisition of information and its processing are referred to as *learning* styles – and whilst there are a range of definitions, that which best summarises the current literature is given by Ladd and Ruby (1999:363):

> *"...characteristic cognitive, affective, and physiological behaviours that serve as relatively stable indicators of how learners perceive, interact with, and respond to the learning environment".*

The recognition that groups of individuals learn in differing ways and that these learning styles impact greatly on educational outcomes is essential in developing rounded and inclusive teaching strategies for employability. A single delivery method (and material structure) is necessarily exclusionary and will clearly be detrimental to the integration process as a whole (Heffernan et al., 2010).

The understanding of differing students' styles of learning and the way information is processed is crucial for a range of reasons; importantly however research has indicated that matching the teaching and learning style increases information retention. Additionally the same information is applied more effectively; the students have a more positive attitude towards the subject and generally are higher achievers (Charkins et al., 1985: Felder and Silverman, 1988; Boles et al., 1999). Clearly this is important for the effective delivery of employability skills. That is not to say that learning styles are universally accepted or adopted, some researchers have argued a lack of evidence for the view that matching teaching and learning styles is significant (Robotham, 1999). Others have suggested that a students' learning style is not fixed and is malleable enough for educators to enter into a versatile learning style exchange with the learner (Smith, 2001).

These dichotomous views, so common in cultural and socio-educational research, do nothing to devalue the impact that learning styles potentially have on both the learner directly and the learning process more generally. The existence of the debate necessarily warrants further and more detailed research and for the current discussion the impacts, however significant, should be treated as both tangible and important.

What is inescapable is the notion that examining the way individual students enter into the information transfer process, and the way that this uptake affects the teaching mechanisms at play, is fundamental to a more effective approach. Thus it is issues of measurement which become an important focus of research, and there have been a number of measures developed which aim to examine students' learning styles. Three main measures have been the subject of the majority of the academic debate:

- *The Grasha-Reichmann Learning Style Scale (Reichmann and Grasha, 1974)*
- *The Kolb Learning Style Inventory (Kolb, 1996)*
- *The Soloman-Felder Index of Learning Styles (Felder, 1993; Soloman and Felder, 1999)*

The differences between these three scales are subtle and beyond the scope of this chapter to examine in any great detail. However, for the research purposes a scale was required which had as its main focus comprehensive and parsimonious elements of learning; for which the Soloman-Felder Index was the most suitable. Recent research examining the applicability of various scales found the index to be internally consistent and valid for a range of students, something not often found with learning styles (Hosford and Siders, 2010).

The Soloman-Felder index consists of four dimensions, made up of 44 discrete-choice questions (see Figure 5.1):

1. The active/reflective (ACT/REF) dimension indicated student preference for information – with active learners preferring actions. Contrastingly, reflective thinkers use introspection to increase information retention.

2. The visual/verbal (VIS/VRB) relates to sense information – and unsurprisingly visual learners prefer visual information and verbal

learners what they hear and read.

3. Sense/intuitive (SEN/INT) relate to the actual information individuals preference. Sense individuals prefer to see things and physically sense them, which intuitive students prefer abstract ideas, relationship links and discovery.

4. Sequential/global (SEQ/GLO) indicates the ability to progress towards full comprehension. The former refers to those who prefer logical and linear processes and the latter to a more holistic approach.

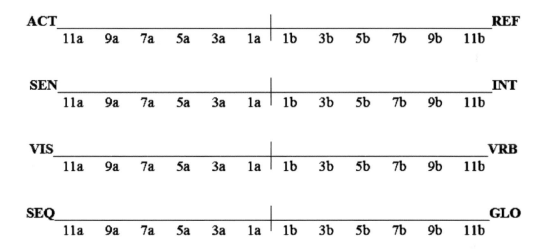

Figure 5.1 Index of learning styles

(Source: Felder and Soloman, 2004)

The differences exhibited by learners across all of these scales should be taken into account when lecturing staff integrate employability skills into delivery; the alternative is inherent bias: whereby some learners will benefit more than others. It is important to note, however, that no learning style is quantitatively (or qualitatively) better than any other;the aim of these sections are to better *understand* learning styles so as to better understand the differences in student cohorts.

Research was undertaken by John White, Juliet Memery and Troy Heffernan at Plymouth Business School, which sought to identify how learning styles varied between students from a University in England and those from a

University in China. Samples were gathered from a single institution from each country, 235 from China and around 350 from England; using a questionnaire developed for the study.

In the questionnaire students answered the Soloman and Felder (1999) learning styles index. As part of this index, students complete 44 discrete-choice questions that when calculated determine their learning style on four continuums. The strength of preference that a student has for a particular learning style construct (e.g. active-reflective, visual-verbal etc.) can be represented by their value on a 23 point scale (-11; +11). A value of greater than plus four or less than minus four indicates that a student has a preference for a learning style on one of the ends of the construct. Hence a value of >+4 on the active-reflective construct indicates that a student is an active learner. Cross-tabs with chi-square tests and independent samples t-tests were used to identify differences in learning styles and preference for teaching aids.

Tables 5.2 and 5.3 report the results of this analysis.

Table 5.2 Learning styles and student country

	Country	N	Mean	Mean Difference	t	Sig. (2-tailed)
Active-Reflective	China	235	-0.174	0.741	2.116	.035**
	England	353	-0.915			
Sensate-Intuitive	China	235	-2.536	-1.007	-2.863	.004**
	England	355	-1.53			
Visual-Verbal	China	235	-2.753	1.423	4.182	.000***
	England	352	-4.176			
Sequential-Global	China	235	0.914	1.923	6.688	.000***
	England	355	-1.009			

Note: *** $p < 0.01$; ** $p < 0.05$; * $p < 0.1$.

There were significant differences between English and Chinese business students for the four learning styles. While Chinese and English students were both more active than reflective, English students were significantly more active in their learning. Further, English marketing students were substantially more visual than their Chinese counterparts. While Chinese students were found to have a slightly more global learning style, English marketing students were slightly sequential.

Table 5.3 Learning styles cross tabulated against country

Learning style	China(%)	England(%)	x^2 (*p*-value)
Active	16.60	25.80	
Reflective	14.90	12.20	7.078
Neither	68.50	62.00	.029**
Intuitive	3.00	14.90	
Sensate	36.60	36.90	23.866
Neither	60.40	48.20	.000***
Visual	43.00	57.10	
Verbal	3.40	4.30	12.813
Neither	53.60	38.60	.002**
Global	25.10	13.80	
Sequential	11.10	31.50	37.284
Neither	63.80	54.60	.000***

Note: *** $p < 0.01$; ** $p < 0.05$; * $p < 0.1$.

Secondly, differences in distinct learning style were examined rather than mean values and here the interest is not only in identifying averages but the proportion of students that had a clear preference for a particular style. Students were argued to have a preference for a specific learning style if they reported a value of greater than (or equal to) plus or minus four on each of the constructs.

As shown in Table 5.3, the differences in learning styles appear more pronounced when displayed in this manner. Striking differences are observable between English and Chinese students; a much smaller percentage of students are active learners in China (16.6% compared to 25.8%).There are also far fewer intuitive learners in China, and Chinese students have a greater predisposition to be global learners while English students are more likely to be sequential learners. Both forms of analysis confirmed that English students are likely to be more active, verbal and sequential than their Chinese counterparts. Additionally, cross-tabulations indicate that in England there are a significantly larger percentage of intuitive students (14.9% compared to 3.0%).

The presence of a significant variance in learning style between university students in China and England means there are inherent issues of cultural difference which are worth exploring in greater depth, and it to these that this chapter will now turn.

5.3 The Role of Culture in Learning

Perhaps a more relevant, though more specialised, definition of culture is by Steve Fenton (2010); the links to learning behavior are clear:

> "Ideas about culture will include myths about the past, beliefs about 'the kind of people we are' and the idea that 'culture', language, dress and custom, define a group." (2010: 12)

More generally, the links between culture, nation and race are hotly debated in the academic literature and it is not the place of this chapter to enter into these technical debates. Rather, it is sufficient to recognise that there is often culturally orientated action, not necessarily consistent for all members of a group but which can influence concrete behaviours (Fenton, 2010). Educationally this can have real and sometimes negative effects; young Latin Americans are often linked to under-performance through negative ethnically ascribed opinions – "...doing well in school, they will be alienated from their ethnic group" (Rivas-Drake, 2008:126).

Many personal differences are explicable to some degree by an individuals' cultural background and, in the context of employability, it is necessary to briefly consider how cultural difference may influence the delivery of skills by UK and Chinese universities.

Cultural patters of thinking, feeling and acting are rooted in common values and societal conventions (Nakata and Sivukumar, 2001). Models have been forwarded which seek to create a typology of culture in the context of learning; Hofstede (1997) conceptualised this as a type of mental programming. For Hofstede (1997:5), culture is a mental facility which is acquired rather than inherited, and is "distinguished from human nature on one side, and from an individual's personality on the other". The proposed typology highlights five continua along which countries differ: power distance, masculinity, individualism, uncertainty avoidance and long-term orientation.

In cultural terms the UK and China exhibit contrasting characteristics in their social traditions and norms (Hofstede and Bond, 1988). For example, China is firmly rooted in Confucian philosophy and values. Confucianism endorses the value of authority, collectivism in society, honour in hard work and the importance of being patient and persevering (Hofstede and Bond, 1988). Western culture, conversely, is rooted in the philosophical ideologies of Kant and Locke (Pratt, 1991). These centre on individualism, freedom of speech and equality of power.

Learning style preferences, as we have seen, vary with cultural values (see also: Holtbrugge, 2010), and so therefore will the uptake of employability skills unless there are elements of innovation of delivery built in. For example, Rodrigues and colleagues suggested that cultures exhibiting higher levels of power distance and authority are more teacher-centred (Rodrigues et al., 2000). Alternatively, cultures with low power distance and equality in authority usually implement more hands-on practices. Yamazaki (2005) rigorously examined the variance in learning styles across a range of cultural typologies and concluded that for each typology there is significant change in the learning techniques and styles. Indeed, cultural difference accounts for a large proportion of change in learning style more generally between Eastern and Western cultures.

However it is also important to note that the differences are not mutually exclusive or supportive. In other words there are a variety of learning styles, a variety of cultural differences and they sometimes interact – the interaction is not predictable, neither is it universal (Young, 2010). What is central to the current discussion is that the way learners interact with material, each other and the learning provider varies with both student *and* cultural difference – something clearly of importance for lecturing staff.

Learning styles in the UK and China are therefore reflected in the historical cultural roots of the country and are also necessarily different. In China students are more likely to consider the teacher as an authority figure and therefore refrain from questioning assertions. This leads to a fairly teacher-centred orientation of lessons in which the emphasis is on the material chosen by the lecturer (Biggs, 1991). There is also a view that Chinese students prefer memory learning, where material is delivered to a more passive audience and is then tested in regular examinations (Chan, 1999). Chinese students are well versed in 'repetitive' (though distinct from rote learning) learning techniques (Biggs, 1991); essential in Chinese scholarship owing to the vast numbers of symbols that must be learnt to master the language. What is therefore confused for passive (i.e. rote) learning, are most often the repetitive techniques employed to fully comprehend a subject (Biggs, 1991; Chan, 1999). In the classroom, Chinese students tend to remain quiet and ordered and wait to be provided with instructions from the teacher (Chan, 1999). The collectivist nature of the Chinese culture is demonstrated by the approach taken by teachers in correcting problems that individuals may have with their work (Biggs, 1991). Students who have failed to complete a task properly may often be used as "an example" by the teacher – for the collective learning of the entire class.

The Western learning approach is also strongly correlated to the cultural heritage which underpins it. The individualistic nature of British society leans more closely towards a student-centred approach. Teachers are conveyors of knowledge, but students are required to learn material for themselves (Biggs, 1991). At the same time, UK students are encouraged to challenge and debate with people in positions of authority, i.e. teaching staff. This is characteristic of a culture with a low-level of power distance (Chan, 1999).

Studies that have tested differences in learning styles via cognitive techniques such as the Kolb learning style inventory (Kolb, 1996), and the Soloman-Felder Index (Soloman and Felder, 1999) have found both similarities and differences in the preferred learning styles of Chinese and Western students. The impact that this may have on the integration of employability skills by lecturing staff should not be underestimated.

The study conducted by White, Memery and Heffernan utilised earlier in this chapter showed that there were significant variances between English and Chinese students in terms of learning styles. Clearly, this impacts on the routes of information uptake and, therefore, the way in which employability skills should be implemented; what strategies are best used will vary with culture.

Extending their previous analysis, the team examined the differences in preference between Chinese and English students with regards to various teaching aids. Illustrated in Table 5.4 are the results from an independent samples t-test for a variety of teaching aids across the two cohorts. Students were asked to indicate their liking for a variety of teaching aids on a five point dichotomous scales with 'Like a lot' and 'Don't Like' at opposing ends of the scale. Lower scores indicated a high preference for the particular teaching aid. There were significant differences between the two cohorts on six of the nine teaching aids examined.

Table 5.4 Teaching aids and student country

Teaching Aid	Country	N	Mean	Std. Deviation	Std. Error Mean	Sig. (2-tailed)
Videos/DVD	China	193	1.72	.966	.070	.000***
	England	350	2.04			
Case studies	China	231	2.00	.953	.063	.008**
	England	350	2.20			
Group work	China	232	2.72	1.012	.066	.114
	England	344	2.59			
Computer practical	China	226	1.94	1.018	.068	.000***
	England	339	2.28			
Student presentations	China	229	2.35	1.064	.070	.160
	England	338	2.48			
Guest speakers	China	228	2.41	1.085	.072	.072*
	England	342	2.56			
Interaction with local businesses	China	225	1.66	.997	.066	.000***
	England	338	2.68			
Lecture notes	China	232	2.75	1.044	.069	.000***
	England	346	2.16			
Overheads/ PowerPoint's	China	225	2.39	1.064	.071	.881
	England	340	2.37			

Note: *** $p < 0.01$; ** $p < 0.05$; * $p < 0.1$.

The Chinese students have strong preferences over their English counterparts for the use of videos/DVDs in class (Chinese 1.72/English 2.04: .000); Computer practical (Chinese 1.94/English 2.28: .000); and interaction with local business (Chinese 1.66/English 2.68: .000). The English students had a preference for receiving lecture notes (Chinese 2.75/English2.16: .000).

What is inescapable is the fact that students from differing cultures are likely to learn in differing ways, need different emphases placed on elements of an employability syllabus and, also, require significantly different employability aids in helping them to learn.

5.4 Summary

Clearly the process of learning is at least partly cross-cut by culture and traditions. This affects how universities are able to implement and embed employability skills and capabilities into courses. Nonetheless, there may be strategies that complement cultural disparities. These will be explored in later sections. At the same time it is critical to identify whether the meaning of employability across the chosen disciplines also varies because of culture. Both of these issues will be addressed. Chapter 6 will detail the methods applied for the empirical research examined in subsequent sections. The results of the empirical work must be viewed with both discipline specifics and cultural difference at the core.

SUM-UP
- ✓ Individuals arguably learn in different ways, these can be classified into typologies.
- ✓ The learning typology can vary with culture.
- ✓ Any examination of Chinese and UK universities must recognise both learning style and cultural difference.
- ✓ The integration and delivery of employability must therefore recognise these cultural differences.

Section B: Enhancing the Employability of Business School Graduates in the UK and China

The importance of employability skills integration is unquestionably of central importance for universities; as well as a comprehensive understanding of the barriers and differentiation faced between cultures, disciplines and individuals. The first section of this book detailed these theoretical debates and outlined previous research which had identified potential barriers and pragmatic issues with the delivery of these skills. The second section, consisting of four chapters, details the methods and results of a major research project examining employability in both China and the UK.

6 Methodology

Previous research has suggested that there are potential differences between what makes a graduate employable across subject disciplines. Simply, what a new employer expects from an individual varies according to the particular profession; albeit within the same broader discipline (i.e. marketing, finance or human resources). Not only are there disciplinary differences but also issues of culture; employability skills and their integration naturally vary with cultural differences. Consequentlly, the strategies teaching staff employ will also vary. This chapter will provide an overview of the methods utilised in a major research project in the UK and China which sought to examine these factors in greater depth. The results from this primary research exercise indicate that, whilst there are significant similarities between both countries and across disciplines, it is more subtle differences which highlight the importance for creative and dynamic teaching strategies and supportive processes; these issues will therefore be explored in greater depth in the following chapters.

6.1 Research focus

The concept of employability emerged from the literature as a central concern for university education providers, consisting of the personal skills and attributes required by employers. There have been attempts to model the individual components which constitute comprehensive employability factors both in the UK and in China (see Chapters 2 and 5). However as well as cultural variance there is also significant variance between discipline specifics, something explored in some depth in Chapter 3.

A research project which sought to explore these issues across all disciplines would be overly broad and lack the required focus for reliable and valid results. Business as a significant entity within the academy, however, is well placed to inform the whole. High numbers of international students at most stages make cross-cultural comparative analyses possible and relevant. Additionally, strong links with industry (which are the foundations of university led business teaching) serve to clarify the importance of employability skills by linking employer (industry) and university needs. No other discipline so acutely links students at all stages with industry (something recently recognised by the Department for Business, Innovation and Skills, 2012) and so the importance of high levels of interaction and embedding are clear, as are the teaching strategies required when delivering them.

The three sub-sections of the business discipline selected in this instance, marketing, finance and human resources are themselves indicative of the wider business discipline. Similar reasoning applies to these three sub-disciplines as for the whole, if not more acutely. The links to industry for students in these three areas are fundamental to the successful completion of a course and being prepared for a competitive workplace. That is not to make an argument for other sections of the academy being less in need of employability integration – merely that as an illustrative case, the sections described in the coming chapters display acute and, more importantly, clear elements. The results presented here are therefore more widely applicable than to merely the sub-disciplines examined; and the recommendations made have relevance to other areas of the university sector.

Formed around this framework, the aims of this study were twofold: firstly to identify *what* specific skills and capabilities (employability attributes) were desired by employers of the differing sub-disciplines. Secondly, research which identified relevant strategies for embedding these attributes into the discipline course material. Both of these elements are necessarily cross-cut by issues of cultural difference (see previous chapter) and the similarities and differences between the UK and China were also explored.

Given the literature gaps which emerged the research questions which are addressed in the following chapters, using the methods given in these sections, are:

1. What combination of skills and capabilities (i.e. employability attributes) are important to employers of marketing, accounting/finance and human resources graduates in the UK and China?

2. How can stakeholders of these marketing, accounting/finance and human resources graduates implement strategies for providing students with the required combination of skills and capabilities?

6.2 Research methods

In order to address these research questions coherently and with high levels of both reliability and validity to the resulting data, it is the selection of appropriate research methods which is central. The more traditional 'paradigm wars' between qualitative and quantitative orientated methodological approaches has been superseded by a more pragmatic focus on selecting the most suited method to answer the specific research questions in a particular instance (Brent and Kraska, 2010; Williams and Vogt, 2011). The research questions given above were developed from the employability literature, which had shown that there was a need for a deep and comprehensive understanding of the linking of needs between employers and graduates; and the differences between cultures.

Methods commonly associated whth qualitative enquiry were thought to be more suited to extracting the richness of data required in this specific case (Berg, 1989). Levels of interpretation are inherent in these data which enable a greater understanding of areas of previously unknown social interaction to emerge (Creswell, 2007). For these reasons a three stage process was designed which was then adapted for use in both the UK and China – see figure 6.1.

Figure 6.1 Research methods

Most appropriate in the current context are notions of *all* of the researchers being implicit in the research process, from interview through to analysis and examination; and so reliability across the series of sections remained high. Qualitative interviews were deemed the most appropriate method of collection and allowed for rich and detailed data to be collected from knowledgeable individuals in the field of employability. In total over 60 interviews were conducted, both in the UK and China, and these data were then analysed by research teams from the two countries. All of the interviews were conducted in the native language of the interviewee and analysed in the same language by the teams. This process was conducted in the social sciences CAQDAS package NVivo, which assists in the sorting of emergent themes into coded responses for subsequent analyses. On completion of each analysis the emerging employability attribute was sorted and placed underneath a wider, more general category. The total of these categories represents a matrix of the skills and capabilities employers expect when recruiting. These matrices are reported in chapters 7, 8 and 9 in tabular form and are presented for both the results from the UK and China.

6.2.1 UK: methods and analysis

The primary research process in the UK followed the sequential stages shown in figure 6.1, allowing for the findings from each stage to inform subsequent elements.

The first section consisted of in-depth interviews with employers responsible for recruiting marketing, accounting/ finance and human resources graduates into their businesses. On completion of the analysis of these data, each employability attribute was placed into a logical matrix (as described above) and stage two then sought to identify relevant strategies that educators and policy makers could apply to university level courses. Interviews at this stage were conducted with educational professionals; it was felt that data gathered at this stage (the experience of lecturing staff in delivering strategies) would be representative of a 'shopping list' of ideas for collation into the analysis. It was also at this stage where resources and documentary evidence were collected and utilised wherever possible. In the third and final phase, experts in the field of employability were interviewed in order to assess strategies which enhance the lecturing evidence collected at stage two. In general, these were experts from universities in the UK and had been tasked by their institution to improve the employability prospects of graduates. A further, final, stage of documentary analysis was also undertaken.

6.2.2 China: methods and analysis

The methods employed in the primary research conducted in China followed the format given in figure 6.1 and those employed in the UK. These stages were also conducted in series to allow for the results to inform the subsequent analyses. Again, the first stage consisted of interviews with employers responsible for the employment of graduates in the three sub-discipline areas

in order to assess the typology of attributes in the Chinese workplace. The results from these organisations were subjected to content analysis whereby latent codes were sorted into emergent themes. It is these themes which represent the key employability skills and attributes which employers in the Chinese market value most. All of these interviews were conducted in the interviewee's native Mandarin, as well as being analysed in the same language by Mandarin speaking academics.

In both China and the UK focus groups were undertaken with the objective of ascertaining the perceived importance of the employability attributes formed in the first stage. Additionally, it was felt that this was a potential source which would boost the resulting data relating to teaching strategies, and which would enhance the employability skills integration from a student perspective.

Due to the nature of the research processes in both countries the most appropriate selection method was snowball sampling – where one expert respondent suggested others, and so on (Berg, 1989). Whilst there are deep rooted (and fierce) debates in the social sciences around sampling procedures and generalisability (see for example Williams (2003)), in instances of qualitative research with relatively small populations and studies seeking exploratory data, it is these convenience based samples which are the most appropriate. It is worth noting that the amount of data collected was significant, over 60 interviews, and so the limitations imposed by the sampling method are significantly reduced.

6.3 Summary

This chapter has outlined the philosophy behind, as well as the pragmatic approach to, the methods utilised in order to rigorously address the research questions which emerged from the literature on employability. The major primary research exercise was undertaken in both the UK and China and sought to firstly identify what combination of skills were important to prospective employers and, secondly, to highlight strategies to integrate these skills into university modules, programmes and the wider teaching culture.

A three-stage qualitative interview methodology was proposed which enabled deep and rich insights to be gained into a previously under-researched social phenomenon. The actual primary research conducted across the UK and China consisted of over 60 of these interviews and therefore represents a significant qualitative study. Though clearly there are some limitations on these data, resulting from the sampling and interview procedures followed (as in any research), the results which are outlined in the subsequent chapters of this book represent a comprehensive analysis of employability skills in the UK and Chinese business sector. What emerged from these data are the striking similarities and differences that exist between generic and specific employability skills and between the appropriate employability elements in the UK and China.

6

Methodology

SUM-UP

- ✓ Interviews conducted with employers of graduates in Marketing, Finance, and HR (UK and China).
- ✓ Interviews conducted with lecturers in Marketing, Finance, and HR (UK and China).
- ✓ Interviews conducted with employability experts and students – with document analysis when relevant (UK and China).
- ✓ The results are therefore a 'pick and mix' of strategies which can be used by lecturers in their own discipline.

7 Results A: The Marketing Discipline and Employability

In the previous section, the methods that were used in the collection of data for this book were outlined. This chapter describes the findings of research conducted utilising these methods in the context of the marketing discipline. The chapter specifically refers to interview data collected from marketing employers, lecturers, students, employability experts and general stakeholders. Key skills and capabilities expected of graduates by employers will be presented alongside potential strategies for embedding them into courses. These strategies are necessarily split between those referring to teaching staff, course materials, abilities and cultural elements; it is left up to the reader to examine these strategies in relation to the literature given in the preceding chapters.

7.1 Marketing

Marketing is a business oriented discipline which blends creative innovation with complex analytical skills. The Chartered Institute of Marketing – the leading body for the UK's marketing industry – defines the discipline as the management process responsible for identifying, anticipating and satisfying customer requirements. In 2004/05, approximately 4.5% of all graduates progressed to work in marketing (Gedye and Chalkley, 2006). Those in the profession can choose, in general, to specialise in the sub-disciplines of marketing research, communications, public relations, strategic management, international marketing, advertising and branding, direct marketing, events organisation and database marketing. In some cases, these sub-disciplines have become industries in their own right, for example, marketing research, public relations, advertising and events management.

Marketing as a degree discipline aims to create graduates with clear and concise communicative skills which are relevant in the current workplace. At the core of the subject are the specific and detailed strategies employed by marketing professionals; and so graduates are able to receive a more specialised education than those selecting a more generic business pathway. Marketing graduates are suited to a number of diverse job markets, including (but certainly not limited to) the sub-disciplines given above. Often the skills sought by employers centre on problem solving, creative enterprise skills and team working.In keeping with the other two disciplines which follow this chapter, marketing graduates must be prepared for an ever increasing and competitive job market and therefore must be given the skills needed in order to be both innovative and employable. It is the identification of these skills which forms the rest of this chapter.

7.2 Marketing employability in the UK

Firms employing marketing graduates in the UK were interviewed in face-to-face and telephone interviews, in each case the interviewees being chosen through a combination of convenience and snowball sampling. Respondents were asked to discuss the most important qualities and skills they required from graduate employees. The importance of each attribute was cross-checked for validity using a follow up question which asked the interviewees to rank their answers. Each interview lasted approximately 30-45 minutes, with the face-to-face sessions recorded using a digital voice recorder.

From these interview data, a total of eight clear themes emerged relating to the skills and capabilities expected of graduate students in the marketing arena. A number of these attributes had sub-attributes:the table overleaf (table 7.1) details the expectations that marketing employers had of new recruits. Each of the attributes is shown in order of importance based on the follow-up question put to the interviewees; these are now detailed (direct quotes are given in *italics*).

7.2.1 Communication

Communication in both written and verbal formats was considered by the interviewees to be the most important attribute a marketing graduate could display. The role of a marketing professional varies from one company to the next and is not as clearly defined as, for instance, the role of an accountant or purchasing officer might be. Marketing as a discipline is seen as having a broad base and could include marketing communications, product marketing or commercial marketing. However, all respondents were clear that communication skills were a vital attribute for all graduates:

"The marketing/commercial graduate needs to be very presentable very communicative and a very, very fast learner."

There were three sub-attributes which split communication and which were seen as important: information transfer, networking skills, and foreign language abilities.

Information Transfer

Having good verbal and written skills such that information is transferred appropriately is vital in a marketing role. This is especially true of those aiming to work in any of the communications disciplines where interpersonal skills are paramount:

"If they [the candidate] have strong interpersonal skills we can pass on a significant amount of knowledge... I would expect them to have knowledge of dealing with such a variety of people."

Table 7.1 Classification of employability attributes desired by UK marketing employers

Dimensions of Employability Expected by UK Marketing Employers	Sub-Dimensions (i.e. Attributes)
1. Communication	a. Information transfer b. Networking c. Foreign language skills
2. Team Working	
3. Problem Solving	
4. Work Ethic	a. Willingness to learn b. Motivation
5. Desireable Persona	a. Self aware b. Confidence
6. Customer Focus	
7. Core Skills	a. I.T b. Numeracy c. Literacy
8. Leadership	

Networking

Falling within the broader communication category, networking ability also had strong links with team working (a category detailed later in this section). Marketing is a position which consists of considerable and prolonged contact with other people in differing departments within a single company. The roles are also usually outward facing and therefore personnel were expected to have a good standard of contact with external companies, suppliers and customers. All of the respondents acknowledged the importance that the ability to network has:

> *"Usually you want someone who can go out and network and get on with other people in the company"*

> *"A good marketing person has the ability to pull in the right people when they need them".*

Foreign Language Ability

The ability to communicate effectively was clearly linked to the ability to communicate in more than a single language, and any additional languages were seen as a distinct advantage in the marketing profession:

> *"Communication skills are critical, as are networking skills… a foreign language is advantageous"*

POTENTIAL STRATEGIES -1.Communication

- In-class presentations undertaken by the students on various aspects of marketing to encourage the delivery of information to larger audiences.
- In-class role play to practice communicating between different types of student.
- Real life consultancy projects with organisations to provide first-hand experience of business life, with regard to transferring information and networking across the organisation.
- Guest lectures from respected practitioners to discuss aspects of industry, demonstrate the art of presentational communication techniques, and practice networking within the business world.

7

Results A: The Marketing Discipline and Employability

- Employer 'question time' presentation sessions to enable students to ask questions and network with practitioners of marketing.
- International contact 'buddying-up' system to increase information transfer across cultures and to encourage the development of second languages.

7.2.2 Team working

The ability of a graduate to work as part of a team was clearly valued and related closely to high levels of communication skills. Graduates were seen to be the building blocks for the future management of a company and possessing the skills to progress through the business were thought extremely important.

"Team working is valued very high – they are expected to lead the development of marketing strategies"

"Team working is absolutely critical"

POTENTIAL STRATEGIES – 2. Team working

- Team-based simulation games designed to allow the students to experience group decision making (e.g. Flux Business Game)
- Extra-curricular team consulting projects with real-life business organisations.
- Team-working residential courses (e.g. commando, team activities, sports etc.) to encourage students to appreciate the importance and progress that can be made by working as a team. Similarly, such activities require students to develop trust and commitment - essential ingredients in team based situations.
- Group based assessments, from team presentations of material through to more innovative team exercises such as developing collaborative tender practice.

7.2.3 Problem Solving

The marketing professionals interviewed placed a high relative importance on the graduate ability of demonstrable critical thinking, as well as highly developed problem-solving skills. During the interviews it became apparent that, when recruiting, company managers assumed attributes were present simply because the candidate had a degree. Included in these skills were problem solving, basic IT skills, numeracy skills and a good command of English.

A more detailed discussion of these attributes however revealed that amongst marketing graduates, some employers felt that a few of these core skills needed to be more highly developed; problem-solving was one such example. The level of problem-solving assumed was high and graduates were simply not seen as attaining such a level. The reasons posited for this discrepancy centred on the speed at which the industry progresses, as well as the need to apply appropriate methodologies for innovative solutions at all levels. Typical comments included:

"Problem solving, again you automatically expect that from a graduate"

"They need to be aware of the steps to go through to solve a problem"

POTENTIAL STRATEGIES – 3.Problem solving

- Working case studies/stories; where the student is expected to formulate a solution to a real-life marketing problem experienced by an organisation. This can also be conducted in teams to develop team working in group based situations.
- Role playing scenarios to encourage the student to address problems from different business angles. An example may include resolving customer problems within a customer service department, or working towards a tight deadline.
- Mini KTP's (Knowledge Transfer Partnerships) where the student is expected to solve a real life business problem over a short period of time by applying the skills learned during their course. Again, partnerships involve the university, the student and an employer. This provides students with real-life experience of working in business teams.
- Examinations of consumer behaviour and strategy – developing tactics to increase, for example, repeat business from first –time clients.

Clearly, graduates are recruited by companies based on their potential and not solely on specific and measureable task skills. Overall, employers wanted to see evidence of this potential, and to this end two key sub-attributes were identified: motivation and willingness to learn.

Motivation

Unsurprisingly being motivated to do a particular job was seen as important. A willingness to engage comprehensively and to take a project further was seen as synonymous with being motivated.

> *"We look for people who are highly motivated with a lot of self-belief"*

> *"Self-motivation is more important when you are working in a small team. You need to be self-motivated and proactive as well and take the initiative"*

Willingness-to-Learn

Whilst being motivated enough to do the job well was seen as critical, employers recognised that specific skills could be learnt and, in many ways, it was beneficial to instil in graduates the company ethos and practices. Similarly, being flexible to change was also seen as important:

> *"They have got to want to learn"*

> *"Primarily [we are] looking for [a] graduate with a proven ability to learn and to learn new concepts".*

> *"Especially with marketing you have got be flexible – you can't assume that what you used to market a product a year ago is going to work today."*

> *"Willing to learn – that's very important"*

POTENTIAL STRATEGIES – 4.Work ethic

• A well-defined course outline booklet with proposed findings/outcomes so that students understand the format of the course and thus remain motivated to its completion. This encourages participants to feel confident about the course direction – and their own target learning outcomes.

- Interactive classroom sessions that allow students to participate in the lesson and to voice their opinions, feelings and concerns. This is believed to empower students to have opinions, thus motivating them and increasing their willingness-to-learn.
- Competitive (group-based) projects where students are able to compete against each other. Students are motivated to be the best team and therefore exercise a willingness to learn in completion of this goal.
- The integration, at this stage, of concepts of life-long learning and continuing professional development for differing career stages.

7.2.4 Desirable persona

Less specific, but still central to the employers, were certain personality traits which were expected in prospective employees. These included high levels of self-awareness and confidence.

Self-Awareness and Self Confidence

A graduate having and understanding their specific personality traits and how these relate to their role as an employee was important to employers. At the same time, however, there was a need to be confident and to possess an element of self-belief – though of course there was a thin line between being realistic and being confident.

> *"The qualities that stand out for me here are having self-awareness and confidence"*

POTENTIAL STRATEGIES – 5.Desirable persona

- In-class role play activities to build student confidence and to raise self-awareness. It was felt that when students play the character of somebody else, they begin to understand more about whom they are and where their strengths and weaknesses lie.
- One-to-one appraisals with the course instructor to review progress and set targets for future personal achievements. This allows students to have a better

understanding of who they are and where they could improve in the future.
- In-class presentations undertaken by students to build confidence and self-belief. Experience of speaking to audiences is felt to be important for raising the confidence of less-assured students.
- End of course reflective self-appraisal for students to evaluate their own progress, their personality traits and any improvements required for the future.
- Life skills development seminars held as extra-curricular to aid students to develop the most important aspects of their character and those aspects that remain less developed.

7.2.5 Customer focus

Several of the interviewees stated that, for them, the distinction between numbers of the attributes was blurred. The pre-requisite of a career in marketing is that a graduate needed advanced communication skills and, by implication, if he or she possesses these skills then other essential skills are also likely to be evident.

To be successful in marketing, graduates needed to be inherently comfortable with people at all levels, both internally and externally (with suppliers and customers). Depending on the marketing role in question, putting the customer first was seen as very important.

"In a marketing role customer orientation must be high"

POTENTIAL STRATEGIES – 6.Customer focus

- Consultancy assignments in which students may be expected to undertake a project with a marketing organisation as their customer.
- Report based assignments where the student is expected to produce a report document similar to that expected from practitioners of marketing.
- Business games (e.g. flux etc.) whereby the students are expected to operate as they perceive they would in the external environment (i.e. meeting customer needs etc).
- Guest speakers from external organisations who can discuss their experiences of being customer focused (e.g. perhaps from a customer service background).
- Examinations of consumer behaviour in a wide range of settings.

7.2.6 Core skills

As mentioned in section 7.2.3 there were certain core skills which employers expected graduates to be able to demonstrate as a result of completing undergraduate or postgraduate training; namely numeric, verbal and IT skills.

Numeric

Basic numeric skills are taken for granted,though a level of numeracy required for detailed statistical analyses was not expected. Nevertheless some of the respondents stated that graduates needed to be at a good enough standard to deal with at least spread-sheet style data:

> *"They need to have advanced reporting skills other than just words. A high level of IT – especially numeric and graphic representation of data is needed"*

Literacy

Again, being literate was argued to be inherent in the ability to communicate effectively. This was especially true when presenting word documents and reports.

> *"They have to be able to tick the basic literacy box to pass go"*

IT

The ability to use IT was seen as very important to marketers;to many, an understanding of IT was synonymous with problem-solving. However being able to use basic software packages was critical for the day-to-day functioning of the business. Typical comments included:

> *"I would expect IT literacy to be a given"*

> *"IT skills are a given, someone who is comfortable with computers is important; it's another tick in the box."*

> *"You would expect students to be familiar with Microsoft products – Word and spread-sheets"*

> **POTENTIAL STRATEGIES – 7.Core skills**
>
> • Application of various software packages throughout the course to provide students with a good level of IT skills (e.g. Microsoft Office, Adobe, etc.).
> • Use of support technologies to supplement the course (e.g. wiki's, blogs, etc) to encourage students to interact with computer products.
> • Numeracy workshops for students to practice their mathematical skills.
> • In class presentations led by students for them to improve their verbal and literacy skills.

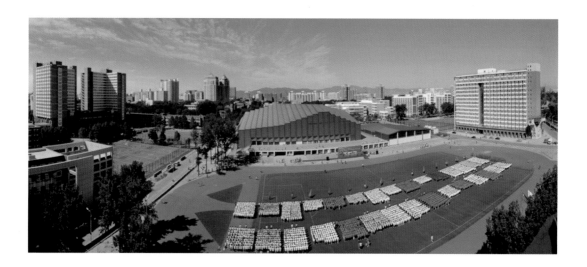

7.2.7 Leadership

A recruit in marketing was viewed as a potential future senior manager or company director, and in this respect a drive towards personal and corporate success was admired. Whilst having motivation was a large part of leadership it encapsulated far more, including the ability to challenge and to be innovative.

> *"Employing marketing graduates of above average IQ and would be capable of becoming the managers and directors of the future"*

> *"We expect them to integrate and innovate...they need to challenge current practices"*

7.3 Marketing employability in China

In the stage of research conducted in China, organisations employing students with marketing degrees were interviewed. Once again, in each case directors or deputy directors of the marketing divisions were questioned in sessions lasting around 30 minutes. Questions covered the most salient skills and attributes that a graduate needed to possess as well as the ranking which was afforded to these attributes.

An analysis of each of these interviews led to the emergence of six main themes; though as before in many cases sub-attributes existed within the wider theme (see below, table 7.2). Each of these attributes is now detailed in order of importance and, in keeping with the previous section detailing the UK, quotes are similarly shown in *italics* and strategies to be employed for integrating these attributes are shown separately for reference.

7.3.1 Executive ability

In a rapidly expanding and developing market, increased competition means that companies pursue higher rates of growth. Such increases require employees to have the highest executive capability; positions in marketing

Table 7.2 Employability skills salient to Chinese marketing employers

Dimensions of Employability Expected by China Marketing Employers	Sub-Dimensions (i.e. Attributes)
1. Executive Ability	a. Problem Solving b. Creativity
2. Communication	a. Information collection and analysis b. Persuasive ability c. Information transfer
3. Desirable Persona	a. Reliable b. Trustworthy
4. Working Enterprise	a. Achievement oriented b. Diligence
5. Professional Knowledge	a. External awarness b. Subject knowledge
6. Adaptive Skills	a. Stress management b. Flexibility to change

especially are required to define targets and to achieve them using a mix of problem solving, creative thinking and flexibility.

Problem solving

The performance of marketing staff was believed to be linked to quantitative sales targets, something not present in the UK analysis. Such outcome focused targets mean that strategies are frequently not specified for marketing sections of large businesses;having someone who endeavours to complete a job above anything else was desirable. Employers also specified the impor-tance of creating and maintaining accurate and achievable goals and targets – a culture of task execution.

"I like the person who can get things done. We have a popular

saying to describe a person: the good cat is the one who can always catch the mice, no matter whether the cat is white or black (Mr. Deng Xiaoping's popularised saying)."

Creativity

The dynamic and developing market in China requires people to be good at both thinking and acting on their ideas; states of change within this specific market need different employability skills to those required in the UK. Many managers described the importance of identifying niche markets(and therefore the creative process) when developing new ideas, exploring insights and working flexibly towards goals for success.

"...the market is (composed of) people, and people are always changing. Therefore the marketers should think and act creatively and flexibly. Otherwise those graduates should do engineering rather than marketing."

"...we always say, a wise vision guides a gold mine"

POTENTIAL STRATEGIES – 1.Executive ability

- Systematic planning of students' targets for study and research from the beginning of a module and then throughout. Interactive strategies maintained between the lecturing staff and the student, as well as incorporating periodical review and guidance.
- Work-based learning and internship opportunities should form part of module material, a bridge between academic and practice-based knowledge. These should ideally focus on real applications of marketing theory to build executive abilities.
- The incorporation of inter-disciplinary elements to course reading and in assessments; in order to broaden students' knowledge outside of the core subject material. Mixing module teams into business wide scenarios, for example. These should also integrate technology developments such as Gantt Chart design or chain method analyses.

7.3.2 Effective communication

Students are provided with large amounts of information and need to communicate it effectively for successful decision-making and selling. Graduates in this case were also required to display high standards of oral and written communication skills for persuasion, client relationship management and forecasting in business. Employers highlighted the need for well developed all round communication skills in marketing; specifically those which were linked to information collection, analysis and transfer alongside persuasion skills.

Information collection and analysis

The ability to collect and analyse market information through both formal and informal channels was seen as important, as was the ability to analyse information systematically.

> *"Some graduates speak with no points and act with no points too. I believe they don't know how to find information and find points from that information."*

Persuasion

In Chinese culture great importance is placed on Guanxi (networked people connections) and on social networks. An excellent graduate was described as being an individual who was good at developing connections through differing networks composed of different social classes, as well as an individual who could persuade a prospective client in an acceptable manner for their social class.

> *"...talking with clients is a kind of art. I want new staff who can use their mouth for pleasing clients [interesting conversation] not just for eating food. Such ability is a kind of person-to-person Guanxi building, making your client accept your ideas and service."*

Information transfer

Oral and written skills were indicated by marketing managers as key attributes of qualified applicants looking for positions in marketing. Oral skills included the accuracy of a statement, the emotional influence used and the persuasive ability.

> *"...graduates should be good at both oral and written skills. Talking about the oral skills, the customer actually starts to evaluate your product and your company in the first words with your salesman. If a high quality company can make their product high quality, certainly it can make it presented [by a salesman] very well....Although witten skills of a salesman are less important than the oral to customer, it is still important for a salesman to have when it is needed. Written skills are also quite important internally to demonstrate that [they] have management potential."*

POTENTIAL STRATEGIES – 2.Communication skills

- Group self-assessments, including an analysis of the roles and responsibilities of team members. Such exercises must have high levels of oral and collaborative presentations to both peers and staff.
- Marketing scenarios to be worked through linked with extra-curricular bodies such as student unions or clubs and societies – collaborative problem-solving with individuals outside of the specific module/programme.
- Guest lectures and working seminars from leaders in communicative fields; public speakers, analysts as well as professional writers and communicators outside of marketing.
- Less formal assessment criteria which can incorporate less rigid communication skill demonstration. These could potentially include the attendance and facilitating at an academic conference, the assistance of visiting scholars in their work as well as others.

7.3.3 Desirable persona

Environmental business ethics in manufacturing have been the source of a number of national incidents.In the service industry in particular being ethical is a central concern. Marketing managers placed a high level of importance on having responsible and trustworthy staff. Whilst employers stated that personality characterstics such as these are often formed earlier than university education, there were certain elements which could be developed to enhance the overall employability of graduates.

Responsibility

The term responsible was defined in this case as an individual who could be held accountable to internal work partners as well as to external business customers.

> *"signing a contract and [selling] products is not the end of the marketing process but half-way. Staff should still be responsible for all consequences related to it."*

> *"we never encourage some so called clever salesman who will take advantage of the internal information for expanding his sales records and crossing the market boundary of other colleagues."*

Trustworthiness

The trustworthy attribute described by marketing managers focused on the ability of graduates to foster trust amongst customers; maintaining a network of relationships was essential to continued success.

> *"A good salesman may not rely on knocking on the door of a customer everyday, but on the stable customer network. The network, you know, built by trust."*

POTENTIAL STRATEGIES – 3.Desirable persona

- The design, collaboratively, between supervisor and students, of a code of ethics and set of regulations for continued work. These should reflect the best working practice as well as strict regulatory controls for academic work. Such creative input should also reflect the theories learnt around ethical and honest practice.
- Activities which extend the basic standards of university guidelines into comprehensive marketing guidelines. These could be formulated utilising real-world documentation from business.

> - Meeting-groups incorporated into course delivery – face-to-face meetings with professionals to discuss their experiences of ethical practice and career development. These sessions should reflect the importance of a strong perceived image.
> - Self-assessments – students should be encouraged to examine their own working practice and to highlight positive and negative aspects with regard to desirable marketing traits.

7.3.4 Working enterprise

Marketing-qualified graduates were evaluated as being enthusiastic to reach successful outcomes and to work hard towards success for themselves and others in the business. The motivational element of this enthusiasm was important to employers, who also highlighted the impact that team working had on both target attainment and the desire to succeed.

Achievement oriented

Marketing managers believed that groups of graduates were either driven by successful achievements or motivated by external incentives.

> *"They may harvest nothing if [s/he] doesn't have a strong willingness for achievement. For a graduate to do the marketing they must have strong desire to win, have passion to work. That is where motivation comes from."*

Diligence

All marketing managers suggested that having diligence and patience were just as important as a desire to succeed in marketing posts. They believed that no one could succeed in marketing without diligence and patience.

> *"...at the very beginning I may give some very simple or tedious work to test the ability of graduates, such as collecting feedback from hundreds of customers by phone calls, making hundreds of photo copies...later you will find that not everybody can do it well."*

POTENTIAL STRATEGIES – 4. Working enterprise

- Short sessions which identify, engage and complete competitive activities based around academic success; for example applications for further scholarships, competitions and university centred awards. These sessions should engage national, regional and local excellence.
- Similarly, sessions or seminars which cover competitive elements outside of the academy, engaging with student elective processes or poverty alleviation strategies for example.
- Attendance should be encouraged in a formal manner to high profile events with outstanding individuals. These are not necessarily university centric, but could include attendance at Nobel laureate lectures, political figures and such like.
- Holiday period projects –formal recognition of institutionally awarded internships and project funding for students to engage with the development of publications and academic enterprise during holiday periods.

7.3.5 Professional knowledge

All of the interviewees recognised that experience was more important than theoretical knowledge in marketing. Higher education in China had traditionally only arranged limited work-based opportunities for business students, though some masters-level students were able to accumulate elements of industrial experience during their dissertation work. Marketing managers felt that graduates with a good knowledge structure in marketing theories would ease some issues associated with job-hunting and longer-term career development. It was certainly the *application* of such knowledge which was more highly valued by employers.

External awareness

External awareness was defined as the graduate's practical experience in identifying valuable opportunities, according to market changes.

> *"each business has its internal or tacit principles, which are invisible, but people can feel based on accumulation of experience."*

> *"Some people are born with sensitivity to market changes, some others become sensitive by hard practice. But the hopeless*

graduates in this job may have neither one."

Subject knowledge

Graduates also needed theoretical knowledge about the discipline as a whole, often from generic and specific textbooks.

> *"Although the practical experience is quite important to a salesman, the basic theoretical knowledge can help the less experienced people to do the job more systematically and confidently."*

POTENTIAL STRATEGIES – 5.Professional knowledge

- The integration of case study material into in-class sessions from the real business sector. These should encourage the critical evaluation of theoretical knowledge in order to solve real problems.
- Out-of-class marketing assignments should be fed into discussions, presentations and open conversations in the classroom environment, encouraging the complete integration of theoretical and professional knowledge.
- Core skills exercises which prioritise transferrable methodological skills rather than highly specific ones, which are then applicable to a variety of situational tasks.

7.3.6 Adaptive skills

As a result of China's implementation of family planning policy from the early 1980s more than 90 per cent of current students in undergraduate and postgraduate education are from single-child families. The term "post-80s" is frequently used to describe this generation, who grew up in a more economically stable era and are therefore  less used to tolerating tough work and living conditions. The ability to cope with the associated stresses and tensions of a competitive market was therefore specified by employers as a necessary skill.

Stress managment

Graduates were expected to have the appropriate skills in order to best manage their working life whilst they were under pressure. Specifically, graduates should be able to demonstrate the ability to achieve predetermined targets whilst pressurised. Employers cited successful candidates as those with strong levels of perseverance in the face of tight deadlines.

> *"In this [marketing] job the first thing you should do when opening your eyes every morning is to count the remaining volumes of sales left incomplete. We like graduates who can smile when they think about it, rather than calling their parents."*

Flexibility to change

In such a highly competitive position there are many and varied influencing factors affecting each decision. Graduates were expected to put into place contingency plans, as well as being prepared for sudden changes that contradicted their original plans.

> *"In the market, the only thing that doesn't change is changing. I tell my staff that (marketing) life is running, running and running. You have to run as fast as the market changes."*

POTENTIAL STRATEGIES – 6. Adaptive skills

- Documents and sessions run by the university mental health services from the very beginning of programmes, information from these sessions could be built into innovative and understanding assessment schedules.
- Modules which specifically cover work psychology should be offered as electives to all students.
- Freshman seminars – this is an American derived strategy which incorporates the best teaching staff onto an introductory module designed to set out the discipline as a whole – from methodology to working practice and career planning. Those students with a fuller understanding of the wider picture often are more adaptive to future university stresses.
- In-class practice, group exercises whereby students undertake differing roles to

---

7.4 Summary

Marketing is a central and ever developing business sub-discipline which has seen a distinct rise in student popularity throughout recent years. Higher education institutions across the world now routinely incorporate marketing into business courses and run dedicated undergraduate and postgraduate qualifications in their own right. Educators

should incorporate the expectations of employers regarding the skills required of marketing graduates in order for these students to be competitive in the workplace. The interviews with marketing employers detailed in this chapter demonstrate the contrasts between China and the UK in terms of employability focus. Whilst communicative ability was important to Chinese employers, more importance was placed on a graduate's executive abilities. These executive skills encompassed key skills in areas such as problem solving and creative development strategies; both considered central to developing business through marketing.

In the UK, marketing employers concentrated more heavily on the ability of graduates to conform to an existing normative role; be it a team or a department. This contrasted with the Chinese focus on an individual's potential for excellence: raw talent. Whilst such a dichotomy is not necessarily indicative of fundamental differences in culture, it is somewhat surprising given past studies of cultural elements between the two countries. Hofstede (1980) had found that the UK favoured a more individualistic approach to working whereas the Far East and China were often more collectivist, with emphasis placed on group achievements. The results in this instance do not necessarily conform to such a notion; marketers who can fit into a large team-working environment are desired. Nonetheless, competencies demonstrating drive and determination are also important for marketing employers in the UK. Evidence of being able to solve problems and showing a willingness to learn (whilst remaining motivated) was critical. In China it was expected that dedication to an organisation is shown through consistently trustworthy and reliable behaviour.

The two sets of results given in this chapter provide a basis for interesting comparative conclusions. Marketing, for example, often requires intricate knowledge of an organisation and private information; Chinese employers are therefore primarily concerned with employing graduates who can be trusted with this information – and who will, through time, act reliably and responsibly. Loyalty certainly emerged as a key component of Chinese (especially business) culture.

In conclusion, teachers and policy makers in marketing should be aware of the differences between UK Chinese employers' expectations. The interviews in this instance certainly highlighted the need of these stakeholders to identify, apply and evaluate these components of employability using the strategies suggested throughout these sections. It should, however, be noted that marketing is an innovative and fast-moving subject which relies on creative principles, and therefore these strategies are by no means exhaustive and should be added to or developed as necessary.

SUM-UP
- ✓ Employers in the UK and China look for different skills from marketing graduates.
- ✓ Communication skills are fairly important in both countries.
- ✓ Lecturers and policy makers can adapt their lessons to employ some of the strategies provided.

8 Results B: The Finance/Accounting Discipline and Employability

This chapter continues from the preceding section and presents findings from similar research but from the perspective of the finance industry in the UK and China. Interestingly, and as predicted, the results display stark differences from those given in the marketing section, providing further evidence that employability at the course level should differ in provision depending on subject area. As in the last section, key dimensions of employability will be presented alongside sub-dimensions, followed by potential strategies that can be implemented by teaching staff.

8.1 Finance

The finance industry is a multidisciplinary occupational group of monetary based services; simply, its main utility is the management of money. Significant sections of the industry involve banking and accountancy though insurance companies, consumer finance companies, stock brokerages, investment funds and government sponsored enterprises are also represented. In both the UK and China, financial services contribute significantly to GDP; for example, in the UK, it is estimated that the direct contribution of the financial sector in 2008 was nine percent (Haldane, 2010). In China this figure was approximately six per cent (2004 figures, Australian Government, 2005).

In terms of student numbers, in 2011 HESA predicted that, in the UK, approximately seven percent of graduates left university and entered the financial industry (HESA, 2011). In China, the 2001 figures indicate that around five percent of undergraduates were undertaking financial orientated courses (National Bureau of Statistics of P.R. China, 2001). Participants on financial courses are widely sought after throughout the world. The generic skills expected from these graduates (as indicated by CIHE) are shown over the page in figure 8.1.

A Guide for Employers   **Accountancy**

ACCOUNTANCY

A graduate in Accountancy typically will:

- *Be able to critically evaluate arguments and evidence.*
- *Be able to analyse and draw reasoned conclusions concerning structured and unstructured problems from both given data and data that must be acquired.*
- *Be able to locate, extract and analyse data from multiple sources.*
- *Self manage their learning.*
- *Be numerate, including being able to manipulate financial and other numerical data and to appreciate statistical concepts.*
- *Be effective in ICT including using spreadsheets, word processing software and online databases.*
- *Be able to present quantitative and qualitative information, together with analysis, argument and commentary, in a form appropriate to the intended audience.*
- *Have effective interpersonal skills, including the ability to work in teams.*
- *Understanding the contexts in which accounting operates including the legal and social environment, the accountancy profession, the business entity, the capital markets and the public sector.*
- *Understand the current technical language and practices of accounting (for example, recognition, measurement and disclosure in financial statements, managerial accounting, auditing, taxation) in a specified field.*
- *Understand some of the alternative technical language and practices of accounting (for example, alternative recognition rules and valuation bases, accounting rules followed in other socio-economic domains, alternative managerial accounting approaches to control and decision making).*
- *Be skilled in recording and summarising transactions and other economic events, preparing financial statements, analysing the operations of business (for example, decision analysis, performance measurement and management control), financial analysis and projections (for example, analysis of financial ratios, discounted cash flow analysis, budgeting, financial risks).*

Accountancy is concerned with the provision and analysis of information for a variety of decision-making, accountability, managerial, regulatory, and resource allocation purposes. It is practised, in part, within a professional service context. The study of accounting involves the consideration of conceptual and applied aspects, including at least some of the theoretical considerations underlying the subject.

Students are required to study how the design, operation and validation of accounting systems affects, and is affected by, individuals, organisations, markets and society. Such perspectives may include the behavioural, the economic, the political, and the sociological. In everyday speech, 'finance' is often used synonymously with 'accounting' whereas, in accounting and in economics, finance is restricted to the science or study of the management of funds Some students will pursue a professional accountancy qualification on graduation. Others consider the subject to be a useful introduction to the worlds of business and finance. Some students study accounting predominantly as an intellectual pursuit.

Figure 8.1 CIHE guide to employability - accountancy

(Source: CIHE, 2005)

8.2 Finance employability in the UK

In total, ten accountancy firms who employed graduate level students were interviewed and, in keeping with the sampling process employed previously, the person responsible for conducting the recruitment process was selected using convenience or snowball sampling methods. Respondents were asked to discuss the most important qualities and skills they required from graduate employees; their overall personal traits. The relative importance of each attribute was subsequently cross-checked for validity using a follow-up question which required interviewees to rank their answers. The interviews consisted of a mixture of telephone and face-to-face sessions each lasting approximately 20 to 30 minutes. Additional notes taken during the interview gave researchers a more comprehensive feel for data; allowing themes and commonalities between respondents to emerge.

Table 8.1 Classification of employability attributes desired by UK finance/accounting employers

Dimensions of Employability Expected by UK Employers	Sub-Dimensions (i.e. Attributes)
1. Commercial acumen	a. Internal awareness b. External knowledge
2. Customer focus	a. Service quality b. Relationship building
3. Communication	a. Information transfer b. Networking c. Persuasion
4. Team working	
5. Core skills	a. Numeracy b. Literacy c. I.T
6. Desirable persona	a. Confidence b. Honesty
7. Work ethic	a. Motivation b. Willingness-to-learn
8. Personal organisation	a. Project management b. Time management

Analysis conducted using these interview data in the CAQDAS package NVivo resulted in a total of eight themes becoming apparent (see table 8.1, above). In many cases sub-attributes existed within the wider parent attribute and each of these emerging themes is now examined in order of importance, as reported by employers:

8.2.1 Commercial acumen

Many of the accountancy firms interviewed strongly believed that graduates should have a good level of commercial awareness. Specifically, employers reported great interest in graduates able to demonstrate a breadth of knowledge outside their usual academic comfort zone:

> "Graduates need to have a decent understanding of the world of business"

Within this theme a further two distinct sub-categories emerged which clearly demonstrated the need for extended skills: internal awareness and external knowledge.

Internal awareness

Accountancy employers valued the ability (by graduates) to understand how a business operates internally as extremely important. It was felt central that individuals demonstrate a degree of awareness about the role they realistically play within the business. Employers also expected graduates to have an understanding of how they should operate within the respective culture of their organisation:

> "They need to know what their role within the business is. They need to have the ability to realise that they have to be profitable for us"

> "Graduates need to fit the culture! They need to know enough to realise what we're all about."

External knowledge

An awareness of issues relating to the business landscape as *external* to the organisation was an equally dominant theme. Whereas internal awareness focused on the consciousness of internal functions, employers also reported a desire for graduates with a macro-understanding of the industry. Specific emphasis was placed on graduates demonstrating knowledge of wider issues concerning the industry in which they were placed:

"It is very important to us that our employees are genuinely interested in business and commercial issues. We want people to be passionate about the business world"

POTENTIAL STRATEGIES – 1.Commercial acumen

- Providing students with up-to-date business news and resources (e.g. Financial Times subscription) so that they maintain an informed and current understanding of what is happening in the financial/business world.
- Short work-experience practice within a financial organisation.
- Organised vacation work experience within a financial organisation.
- Work based research dissertation/final report undertaken in a financial organisation.
- Preparing and conducting a meeting in differing situations.

8.2.2 Customer focus

The ability to demonstrate a disposition towards customer-related activity was rated highly. Many employers saw customers as being the vital component in the organisational function. Therefore being able to effectively interact, communicate and deal with customers was high on the agenda of many accountancy firms:

"People who come in often don't realise a big part of the job doesn't involve solely using numbers. It involves customers".

Within the broader context of customer orientation, both service quality and relationship building were central:

Service Quality

Within these results *Service Quality* skills refer to the ability of the graduate to make the customer feel special; to provide satisfaction. Several accountancy employers perceived this demonstration of good customer service skill as being synonymous with representing the company well:

"Having ability for customer service is vital. By this we want people with a can-do attitude, who appreciate that our clients deserve the highest level of service"

"We are looking for people that would represent the firm well when put in front of the client. They need to be presentable and articulate".

Relationship Building

The second sub-theme to emerge related to an employee being able to generate, manage and build successful relationships with clients. Although naturally incorporating service quality skills, this theme placed greater emphasis on the longer-term development of contact with customers. Specific attention was given to the generation of relationships and the skills required for their maintenance:

"Do they know how to speak to people, shake hands etc.? The common courtesies required for building long-lasting relationships"

"They need an awareness of how to treat clients in the longer term. This includes knowing how to act when taking them out for meals."

POTENTIAL STRATEGIES – 2.Customer focus

- Case studies that explore the relationship between the financial organisation and client. Students can organise a file of examples of good/bad practice to use in their own careers.
- Business games (e.g. Flux) that encourage students to make decisions in a business context.
- Guest speakers from customer focused backgrounds (e.g. customer service, relationship managers etc.)
- Customer relation courses used to help students to learn the language that is most easily understood by the layman or non-technical customer.

8.2.3 Communication

Another dominant theme emerging from the interviews was the importance of being able to communicate effectively. Whilst directly related to several other key themes (i.e. team working and customer focus), effective communication skills were discussed in differing contexts throughout the interview process. Communicating well was felt to be the ability to converse successfully enough to create a particular result. In this regard, communicating internally as well as with customers was of utmost importance:

> *"The ability to communicate with people is absolutely essential. This is with both our staff and our clients!"*

Given that this attribute included both internal staff and external customer components, three sub-themes emerged from the attribute; information transfer, networking and persuasion skills.

Information Transfer

Within accountancy the ability to relay information to colleagues and to customers is vital, particularly the capacity to communicate complex information clearly, concisely and in a way that does not require technical terminology:

> *"Being able to communicate is important. By this I mean being able to explain complex things to people who are not as technically minded as themselves.*
>
> *"To make an impact with colleagues and clients they must be able to communicate clearly and confidently. They also need to adapt their style to meet the needs of different audiences."*

Networking

The second sub-theme to emerge was the ability to attain and to utilise useful contacts within and outside the business (networking skills). This differed from building relationships in that networking centred on identifying a wide range of contacts, with the potential to build relationships if required. Effective networking included the ability to solve problems:

"Building rich internal and external networks help us to propose effective solutions for our clients".

Persuasion

The third and final sub-theme to emerge from the interviews in this field was the art of persuasion through effective communication, something equally relevant within and outside the organisation. Several accountancy firms suggested that persuading people to see one's own personal point of view saves both time and cost:

"We want people who not only listen and communicate, but who can use their influencing skills to derive a clearer benefit to us."

POTENTIAL STRATEGIES – 3. Communication

- Guest speakers from the financial world to promote good presentational practice and to allow students to practice their networking skills.
- "Get-to-know" financial employer days where employers are invited to meet students. Students are then given a limited amount of time with each representative to network with them (i.e. employer speed-dating).
- International contact 'buddying-up' system to increase information transfer across cultures and to encourage the development of second languages.
- Listening techniques, developing accurate recording.

The ability to work successfully within a team was also high on the agenda of many accountancy employers. Team working overlapped with other required competencies such as effective communication; however employers viewed it as something over and above the ability to listen and talk effectively. Elements of being able to co-operate, show empathy and to mediate were all key functional skills mentioned. The feelings of employers towards team working were clear and cohesive:

"Teamwork is a big part of what we do...this means that we are looking for people who enjoy sharing ideas and discussing issues

with others, and who value the input of other team members."

"Team working is a cliché, but being prepared to help someone is a fantastic attribute to have."

POTENTIAL STRATEGIES – 4.Team working

- Team based assignments (e.g. presentations, reports, etc.) to encourage students to practice working with other people towards a common goal.
- Team working weekend trips (e.g. away days) where students are expected to work with their team to achieve a goal or target.
- Activities centred on extra-curricular participation in developing conference presentations, poster presentations and similar work dissemination.

8.2.4 Core skills

Throughout the interviews, several employers discussed core (or key) skills. These were seen as essential rather than merely desirable in a graduate, and in most cases it was the recruitment process itself which mediated these skills:

"Having a good standard for the core skills is critical"

Of the core skills discussed three were most critical: numeracy, literacy and IT.

Numeracy

Given the nature of accountancy it was unsurprisingly deemed a pre-requisite that graduates were numerate. Interestingly, most of the employers interviewed were unconcerned by the specific *nature* of the candidate's degree, but more in their overall ability to deal with numerical information:

"We do a numeracy test as part of the selection process...numeracy is very important, but we don't need it to be demonstrated through the degree!"

"We look for strong problem solvers who have the ability to analyse

complex numerical information."

Literacy

As with numerical ability, literacy skills were seen as critical. Competence in literacy was seen as a distinct advantage for the discipline: alongside report writing correspondence forms a large part of routine accountancy work:

> *"We want someone with a good grasp of English, someone with good grammar"*

> *"Writing professionally and having a good vocabulary allows some-one to be able to string together some good sounding sentences."*

Information technology

Although less commonly raised than numeracy and literacy skills, several employers put great emphasis on the ability of graduates to use computers and other technological devices. In all cases employers were interested in the routine applications of technology such as email and document management suites:

> *"They need to have a natural aptitude towards I.T. People who are afraid, or don't use I.T, would not fit in here"*

POTENTIAL STRATEGIES – 5.Core skills

- Application of various software packages throughout the course to provide students with a good level of IT skills (e.g. Microsoft Office, Adobe, etc.).
- Use of support technologies to supplement the course (e.g. wiki's, blogs, etc.) and encouragement of students to interact with computer products.
- Writing assignments such as essays instead of traditional "problem solving" projects. This allows finance students to express themselves in ways other than through purely numeric based assignments.

8.2.5 Desirable persona

The personality of a graduate was seen as an important attribute regarding employability. In the context in which it was discussed, having a desirable persona included the attributes an individual displays as part of their overall character. Within the personality of graduates, accountancy employers mentioned two fundamental components: confidence and honesty.

Confidence

A realistic level of self-belief and confidence was seen as an invaluable personality trait in order to successfully represent an organisation. It was generally felt that confidence in their own potential would assist the employee to accelerate faster through the business. However nearly all respondents who discussed this issue stressed the thin line between confidence and arrogance; having a comfortable respect for authority was certainly a requirement:

> *"Confidence is good, but not when it is bordering on arrogance. This is something we do not want in our firm"*

> *"They cannot be overawed by senior colleagues or customers so they need to be confident. But they should know the hierarchy, and respect it."*

Honesty

Accountancy firms were also interested in graduates who showed qualities of honesty and integrity. It was felt that being able to trust employees, especially with sensitive financial information, was of critical importance:

> *"Honesty and integrity is core to our industry, and we therefore look for these values in people."*

> *"You have got to have integrity!"*

> **POTENTIAL STRATEGIES – 6.Desirable persona**
>
> - One-to-one appraisals with course leaders to help students to develop and grow their personality towards that expected of the future role they wish to attain.
> - Student presentations to audiences to build confidence and public speaking ability.
> - Extra-curricular life skills coaching for students to develop desirable characteristics within their personality.

8.2.6 Work ethic

A candidate's work ethic was aligned to the way in which the job was approached, differing from "persona" which related to the general aspects of a graduate's personality. Once again two dominant sub-themes emerged under this category; motivation towards the job and willingness to learn over time.

Motivation

The motivation to achieve within the organisation was seen (unsurprisingly) as valuable, as was an awareness of personal goals. Employers were particularly interested in graduates who showed drive and resilience to problematic circumstances, and who were motivated and focused in achieving these goals:

> *"We are looking for where people are going to end up, where they want...training someone costs a lot of money – it is a risk!"*

> *"We have all faced times when we have experienced setbacks... what is important is how we react to these setbacks and keep motivated in difficult situations."*

Willingness - to - learn

Whilst it is important to be motivated and driven, accountancy employers also required graduates who were realistic about their ability. Thus, demonstrating a willingness to learn was essential in achieving the targets they set themselves. Employers wanted to see graduates who were not only inquisitive about what they do but were also aware of how they learn most productively:

"We want someone who is realistic about their capabilities. Someone who is willing to develop themselves as an accountant and a service provider"

"Someone who asks intelligent questions of themselves and the company – who wants to learn!"

POTENTIAL STRATEGIES – 7.Work ethic

- Providing well defined course documentation with clear learning outcomes so that students can easily follow their progress throughout the programme.
- Actively encouraging an interactive learning environment. For example, working through solutions to financial problems as a group is likely to encourage students to continue learning and stay motivated.
- Self-assessments, frequent opportunities for students to realistically rate themselves against course criteria in order to understand where their strengths and weaknesses lie.
- Guest sessions with company success stories, focusing on personal development, company commitment and individuals characteristics.

8.2.7 Personal organisation

The final theme to emerge from the set of interviews in the UK was the importance of personal organisation. Employers required graduates to be able to manage their own workload and to deliver accurately in a timely fashion. This also included providing work that satisfied a particular level of attainment. Two sub-themes emerged under this category; employers wanted graduates who were able to demonstrate project and time management skills.

Project management

The ability to undertake (to completion) several different tasks at the same time was seen as particularly useful within an accountancy setting, as each member of staff often held a series of accounts:

"We want people who are highly organised and can deal with multiple tasks at once"

Time management

Respondents were interested in individuals who could multi-task and at the same time prioritise to meet deadlines. Time management skills involved a level of advanced planning which is also critical in accountancy; billing often being directly related to time:

"For accountants, all of your time is billable. You need to account for every minute of your day...managing time is therefore vital, as this is how you get money for the organisation"

"Being efficient and able to prioritise tasks is important"

POTENTIAL STRATEGIES – 8.Personal organisation

- Non-flexible yet clearly stated coursework deadlines will teach students to manage their workloads effectively.
- Personal action planning, where the student works closely with the lecturer to plan goals and targets under certain time constraints puts the student in charge of the workload.
- Event management activity in which the students are expected to plan an event from conception to completion. Possible examples may include: visiting a large financial corporation, a guest speaker or seminar, or a class social event. Through this students will develop both their project management and time management skills.

8.3 Finance employability in China

Thirteen Chinese organisations employing graduate level students from finance and accounting were interviewed, predominantly those trading in the stock market. As before, managers or deputy mangers of finance sections were interviewed for around 30 minutes and asked to identify the salient skills necessary for a graduate to demonstrate and to rank these skills accordingly. The results are tabulated below (Table 8.2):

Table 8.2   Classification of employability attributes desired by Chinese Finance/Accounting employers

Dimensions of Employability Expected by China Employers	Sub-Dimensions (i.e. Attributes)
1. Learning, thinking and analytical skills	a. Independent learning b. Logical and analytical
2. Personal organisation	a. Problem Solving b. Project Management
3. Desirable persona	a. Loyalty b. Integrity
4. English language	
5. Communication	a. Internal b. External
6. Working enterprise	a. Achievement oriented b. Prudence c. Team working
7. Adaptive Skills	a. Stress management b. Flexibility to change

8.3.1 Learning, thinking and analytical skills

China's economy has seen rapid growth over the last decade, with GDP increase averaging eight per cent. This rapid expansion has been driven by business growth alongside product diversification. During this period, the economic laws, procedures, policies and standards have been updated accordingly and accounting managers attach great importance to the ability of a graduate to learn continuously and autonomously.

Independent learning

Employers focused on the ability of a graduate to continuously update their knowledge of economic law, regulations, policies and accounting standards.

> *"...the banking [sector] in China is challenged by change. We not only care about what our new staff have learned - that is textbook knowledge mainly. We care about whether the new person can autonomously learn in the future."*

Logical and analytical

Many positions available for graduates were technical, such as basic data collection and analysis. Graduates should therefore have a strong understanding of business and be able to make connections between key relevant factors, drawing them together logically and in an analytical manner.

> *"In many cases, I just found guys doing things without their 'brain' (thinking). I cannot say in which way you could teach them to do things with procedures and with in-depth thinking. The in-depth thinking means you think thoroughly about everything related"*

POTENTIAL STRATEGIES –1. Learning, thinking and analytical skills

- Short-work experiences in financial companies will help students to understand how to learn and think in financial companies, and how to analytically work in the industry.
- In-class research work from supervisors. These are a good opportunity to practice the skills of learning, organisation, thinking and analysis. The ability to approach and solve problems logically and within a given framework are advanced.
- Presentations from experienced financial employers to help students learn how to effectively work in a financial group.

8.3.2 Personal Organisation

Personal organisation in the form of problem solving was desirable in accounting candidates and was described by the managers interviewed as having a broad scope: integrating personal creativity, technical and social skills.

Problem solving

The ability to solve problems in a creative way was fundamentally important to financial managers.

> *"I like people that have the ability for trouble-shooting. You really can't say what specific skills or knowledge are used at that moment. You need to find problems from both accounting books and talking with people. You also need to solve the problem from both [sole] proposals and acceptance of others. It is a sort of comprehensive ability."*

> *"We believe that some graduates who can find new insights in a routine will be good in implementing a task better than others."*

Project management

As all interviewed organisations were leading companies in their industry there were clear internal specifications of roles and responsibilities. Graduates lacking key planning, executing and controlling skills were perceived to cause increased internal conflicts.

> *"To see whether he has some potential in management, I usually ask him to briefly talk with me about what he has done, what he is doing now and what he is going to do. Also I will ask whether there is a problem or a predicted problem. Good people with potential can always speak it clearly. When he can think clearly, he can do it neatly."*

POTENTIAL STRATEGIES – 2.Personal organisation

- In-class team-working exercises aid the integration of organisational skills, in order to reach specified targets students must work together and follow a pre-defined schedule of work. Also incorporated into these exercises should be methods of trend prediction for the future.
- Seminars and practical sessions designed around the use of project management software and tools – including skills such as budget constraints, cost control and planning.
- Real case analysis, whereby students are given real world problems from industry and asked to identify solutions – enabling flexible trouble shooting and prevention skills to be developed.

8.3.3 Desirable Persona

Similar to the interviews conducted in the UK, respondents identified a desirable persona as a key employability attribute – however, in this case broken down into loyalty and integrity. The former refers to graduates' attitudes in keeping business specifics private and the latter to the ability to alter behaviour accordingly.

Loyalty

Loyalty was indicated as the ability of a graduate to be responsible with business information.

> "Such jobs [working in banking] are different from many others. There is lots of information that can only be talked about with the internal person who is predetermined. You know, I can't tell my wife how much money her parents saved in my bank."

> "Any candidate will be declined if he is found of lying in the past, during the application process or in a probationary period. It is predictable that a dishonest person certainly will not keep business secrets."

Integrity

Integrity constituted a candidate's ability to demonstrate honest, sympathetic behaviour and self-discipline.

> *"The slogan of our company for staff is 'honesty is foundation, sympathy is important, regulation stick to, and fraud [will] never do."*

POTENTIAL STRATEGIES – 3. Desirable persona

- Case studies should be presented which represent the negative aspects of individuals within an organisation lacking loyalty. Severe implications for businesses and those involved should be worked through and systems suggested limiting disloyal behaviour.
- Industry standards regarding the regulation of the financial markets should be built into course material and form the basis of sections of assessments.
- Scenarios as part of discussion groups, forming the basis of 'trials' to expand on the moral and legal implications of the market.
- Brain-storming exercises to develop outside the box thought processes.

8.3.4 English language

Linguistic ability was highlighted in the banking sector most acutely as being a central requirement – especially that good levels of English language were to be demonstrated by candidates.

> *"We are an international corporation, speaking and writing in both Chinese and English is a basic requirement for all jobs here."*

POTENTIAL STRATEGIES – 4.English language

- Dedicated English language courses to be made available to all students and to form part of assessments in modules centred on accounting/finance. These courses should be available both in pre-sessional and inter-sessional format.
- More highly specific interactive sessions could be run with accounting professionals examining the use of English as a working language.
- Online blended delivery of English language material alongside Chinese material for greater integration.

8.3.5 Communication

Finance and accounting managers strongly identified good communication skills as fundamental to a highly employable candidate; something further divided into the need for both good internal and external communication.

Internal communication

Effective communication internally was identified as the ability to communicate appropriately with work colleagues in order to better solve problems and to achieve targets.

> *"When we test a candidate's ability for internal communication, we usually give people a tough problem and ask for a solution. Graduates with bad communication skills may suddenly panic about it. However, good ones may keep asking you questions."*

External communication

Communication with external clients was also important:the ability to communicate effectively and with accuracy was identified as paramount.

> *"Being human nature, some people are born outgoing but others are quiet. Staff should speak when needed in an appropriate manner, especially with the client..."*

POTENTIAL STRATEGIES –5. Communication

- In-class oral presentations aid the development of communication as well as confidence; these should take the form of both individuals and groups.
- Presentation of complex material to peers in group sessions, in order to summarise (for example) literature integrated clarity into communication.
- Critical writing assessments, such as analysing industry performance through the media, are important for the development of writing skills.
- Attendance at industry events with high profile speakers, in order to assess the levels required to be successful in professional communications.

8.3.6 Working enterprise

A strong working enterprise was defined by managers as an important indicator of a graduate's potential in future career development. Enterprising ability was identified as striving for excellence within work, prudence and team-working abilities.

Achievement Oriented

Graduates were expected to work hard towards achieving excellence.

> *"A soldier who doesn't want to be a general is not a good soldier. I would say that if new [members of] staff are self-motivated towards excellence, [they] have the potential for a bright future in banking."*

Prudence

Accounting managers highlighted the importance placed on employees to be careful with money and to maintain meticulous records.

> *"A graduate should always be careful when doing the work on their desk, as well as working with people. Success and failure depends on the details you work with."*

Team working

Team working ability was perceived as one of the most important attributes in order to maintain a harmonious business culture within the department. This included all informal communications, the ability to have a friendly manner, the avoidance of conflicts with people, a good balance within the team and shared values.

> *"I evaluate working ability based on their working with others, say, team working. Such people might not certainly be very talkative but may be popular when working in a group."*

> ### POTENTIAL STRATEGIES – 6.Working enterprise
>
> - Award schemes should be explained and individuals encouraged to work towards these competitive recognitions. These are not necessarily work focused and can recognise academic, sporting, social or other extra-curricular activities.
> - Successful and well-positioned individuals from industry should give guest lectures at the institution or students should be able to attend other high profile events to assess strategies for success.
> - Short-term work experience within the industry in question, either as part of a module assessment or in holiday periods with support from the institution.
> - Intra and extra-curricular events involving team members from differing modules but similar programmes to integrate these communicative skills into a broader format.

8.3.7 Adaptive skills

The interviewees recognised that one of the key skills for employability was a graduate who was able to manage the pressure of a working life and also their lives more generally. This was felt to be especially important when an individual was fitting into a new role or a new working environment.

Stress management

The high levels of 'post-80s' individuals, single children who grew up in a financially more stable era and have been criticised for having less resilience, potentially indicates a workforce less prepared for a highly flexible and tough working environment.

> *"A popular weakness of the post-80's is that they don't have experience of frustration and don't know how to deal with it. It happens quite often that graduates may do something stupid when under pressure in work."*

Flexibility to change

Graduates were identified as needing to demonstrate an ability to adapt to change; these changes could include, but are not limited to, the switching from a more social role to that of an employee.

"We believe a good graduate should have the ability to adapt to a new role or a new task. The work doesn't wait for people and we can't wait for new staff to grow up for years."

POTENTIAL STRATEGIES – 7.Adaptive skills

- Opportunities to attend elective courses covering work psychology and stress management for those students who wish to develop strategies to combat mental fatigue.
- Ensuring all course material is current and accurate regarding working conditions and working life; so that students have a realistic expectation of what they can expect. This material should also include information regarding sources of extra-curricular help should it be required.
- Role-play in group sessions whereby students can alter their roles as the session progresses in order to develop flexible and adaptive strategies to work changes.
- Production of realistic and monitored work plans.
- Quick-response tests.

8.4 Summary

The role of financial services in the economy of both the UK and China is fundamentally important – it is therefore also considered a highly respected profession in both countries. The interviews conducted for this research highlight the importance recruiters put on finding suitable attributes in their candidates. It is unsurprising that the processes involved in securing employment in this market are scrupulous, competitive and often require further qualifications. In the UK and China the cost of these further qualifications is often borne by the employers themselves, the investment in a single employee is therefore considerable. Despite these similarities there are some stark differences between what constitutes critical employability criteria across the two countries.

In the UK, employers highlighted the importance of finding graduates with demonstrable commercial acumen alongside a well-developed customer focus. Candidates were expected to possess current and relevant knowledge of the business environment and to have the accompanying interpersonal skills in order to offer a high level of service to clients. The ability to build relationships was also considered central – mainly due to the fact that employees are often required to be client focused at an early stage in their career. The organisational skills required to deal with clients professionally was echoed in the interviews with Chinese respondents. The emphasis in China was for graduates to demonstrate high levels of honesty and integrity in all aspects of their professional lives.

Whilst the emphases may differ, notions of honesty were certainly features of the UK requirements; somewhat unsurprising given the nature of the financial industry. The role that language skills played in employability differed between China and the UK, with the latter placing less emphasis on foreign language skills. The ubiquitous use of English in the business world clearly impacts on the need for Chinese graduates to demonstrate these skills.

In summary, the strategies presented in this section are representative of the needs of employers in the financial industries and therefore represent essential employability skills for financial degree courses. Lecturers and policy makers alike should be advised to employ strategies which address these key issues, though with the encouragement to adapt, develop and utilise innovative techniques in order to meet their own needs and those of their students.

SUM-UP
- ✓ Finance employers in the UK and China look for different skills and capabilities from their employees.
- ✓ Trust and loyalty are more central in all aspects of Chinese business culture, but are also critical in British financial organisations.
- ✓ In the UK, employers focused more on commercial acumen and customer focus.

9 Results C: The Human Resources Discipline and Employability

This section presents the findings of the qualitative interview analysis conducted in the substantive area of Human Resources. Once again the findings indicate notable distinctions between the previous two disciplines in what is expected of graduates when moving into paid employment. Unlike the marketing and finance subject areas, however, human resource professionals tended not to be client-facing and, as such, there was a greater emphasis placed on providing an internal and 'supportive' role. This inherently meant there were a range of personal attributes and capabilities necessary which had not previously emerged.

9.1 Human resources

Human resource management (HR) refers to the business function by which human capital is managed and controlled. The more traditional viewpoint of HR entails a department that deals with hiring, firing, training and other personnel issues. The goal of the HR employee is to contribute towards fostering human resourcefulness through enlightened and cohesive policies in the key areas of education, training, health and employment across all levels of the business. As a critical aspect of the business function, HR has become more central to the service and technological economies which are in turn reliant on human capital performing at its highest level. It is therefore generally considered fundamental to business success to have a competent HR function. Many theories from the human resources literature stem from social psychology, organisational psychology and economics. The following sections detail the findings of qualitative interviews with employers of prospective HR graduates firstly in the UK and, secondly, China.

9.2 HR employability in the UK

In keeping with the other phases of the research detailed in this book, eight employers of HR personnel in the UK were interviewed through a mixture of telephone and face-to-face interviews. Respondents were asked to discuss the most important qualities and skills that they required from graduate employees. The importance of each of these attributes was cross-checked for validity using a follow up question that asked the interviewees to rank their answers. Each interview lasted for approximately 20-30 minutes and was electronically recorded. Notes were taken during the interview aiding the analysis stage, which identified the emerging themes and commonalities between respondents. From the analysis of each of the eight interviews, six salient dimensions of employability emerged from these data (see Table 9.1). As was the case in the previous results sections, sub-dimensions existed within the wider dimension.

Table 9.1 Classification of employability attributes desired by UK Human Resources employers

Dimensions of Employability Expected by UK Employers	Sub-Dimensions (i.e. Attributes)
1. Personal organisation	a. Project management b. Time management
2. Desirable persona	a. Approachable b. Confidence c. Emotionally strong d. Empathetic e. Patience
3. Communication	a. Information transfer b. Persuasion
4. Work ethic	a. Motivation b. Willingness-to-learn
5. Commerical acumem	a. Internal awareness b. External knowledge
6. Team working	

9.2.1 Personal organisation

The most important characteristic that employers would expect from graduates entering a Human Resources role was the ability to demonstrate an advanced level of personal organisation. Several employers emphasised the fact that employees are often expected to manage multiple projects at one time:

"It is no good employing someone who likes to do one job and follow it through to completion before starting the next"

As such, two main competencies were expected of graduates when managing their personal organisation: project and time management skills.

Project management

It was commonly mentioned that in real settings project work results in many and varied problems which need quick and innovative solutions. Employers expected graduates to be able to take projects forward by using their initiative and solving problems as they go. Ultimately each member of the HR team takes responsibility for managing individual projects and therefore must be capable of seeing tasks through to completion:

> *"We need someone who is able to make sound decisions with the information that they have available."*

> *"I would be looking for someone who can show a bit of initiative with situations that cause problems. Knowing the theory, but putting it into the practical situation to resolve it."*

Time management

In addition to managing projects, employers expected employees to demonstrate evidence of being able to manage the timescales attached to individual tasks. As the majority of work requires employees to organise their own deadlines, employers expected strong prioritisation skills.

> *"They [graduates] should be able to juggle projects not only by importance, but also by the duration they need to commit to it."*

> *"Because you have lots of little jobs at the same time, you need to be able to manage your time and prioritise. What is a priority today might not be tomorrow because something has happened."*

POTENTIAL STRATEGIES – 1.Personal organisation

- Strict coursework deadlines to encourage students to meet time-based objectives.
- Introduce personal planning folders so that students are responsible for planning their own time and projects. The use of Gantt charts is a good way of prioritising time management.
- Empower students to organise an event of some description from beginning to end. This could be a seminar, guest speaker, activity day or extra-curricular day out.

9.2.2 Desirable persona

A second strong theme emerging from the interviews was the importance of certain personality traits. As a large amount of the work conducted by HR employees involves contact with other members of the organisation, being able to demonstrate certain personal qualities was seen as an essential part of the job. Specific traits that were discussed included being approachable, confident, emotionally strong and empathetic as well as having patience.

Approachable

One of the responsibilities HR employees have is to provide support for other members of an organisation. Therefore graduates should demonstrate qualities which enable colleagues to confide in them; employers specified the need for evidence of being approachable.

> *"We are a supportive role which requires someone with an aptitude to deliver support"*

> *"You [graduates] have definitely got to be personable...by this I mean likeable. The main thing is that you come across as someone who can be confided in."*

Confidence

One of the main responsibilities of HR employees is to provide support and guidance to managers throughout the organisation in which they work. Often these are senior managers who rely on the advice given to them. Not only do members of the HR team need to have a working knowledge of what they are involved with, they need to be able to deliver their opinions confidently.

> *"Credibility is huge…our managers need to know if they come to you [graduates], you will know what you are talking about."*

> *"They [graduates] need to be able to go to meetings with senior managers at the council and hold their own by talking credibly to senior people."*

Emotional strength

As HR employees play a supportive role in the lives of other members of the organisation it is fairly common for them to be involved with personal aspects of people's lives. It was thought to be very important that graduates were able to remain emotionally strong despite issues that may cause upset.

> *"Sometimes you need to deliver bad news or deal with sensitive subjects that may upset you. You have to be strong…it's a special inner strength."*

Empathetic

At the same time as remaining emotionally strong and being approachable, HR employees are required to manage situations when they are asked for help. When issues are sensitive and the emphasis is on providing support or a solution to a problem, HR employees are expected to demonstrate empathy. In this context, demonstrating empathy is about understanding other people's issues.

> *"Some people think that they don't need other people to relate to them. I am not talking about on a superficial level. You need to be able to put on someone else's shoes."*

> *"Empathy is when an employee may come up to you and give you a story. You need to put yourself in their position and try to make it better – resolve it for them."*

Patience

As HR employees play a supportive role within the organisation more broadly, they are often expected to provide practical advice and guidance. It is important that HR staff remain patient when delivering such guidance and training.

> *"Having someone with the patience to listen and read between the lines. Not allowing people to get frustrated or feel as if they are ignored is something we strive to do"*

POTENTIAL STRATEGIES – 2.Desirable persona

- Use open forum class sessions for students to freely discuss what they believe makes somebody a "good" human resources advisor.
- Use group projects and coursework assignments for students to develop their position within a team. This allows them to work on some of the essential ingredients of a desirable persona, such as empathy and honesty.
- Use role-play in various situations (e.g. disciplinary meetings, hiring/firing, delivering bad news) to help students to develop a range of skills and methods for dealing with difficult personal situations they may encounter.
- Enrol students on extra-curricular professional courses to enhance aspects of their personality salient to an HR position (e.g. counselling courses, life skills courses, etc.).

9.2.3 Communication

The ability to communicate is a vital attribute within the HR profession. As much of the job involves advising, supporting and guiding members of the organisation, it follows that being able to communicate ideas is essential. One of the key issues is that HR employees have to have contact with a wide range of people throughout the organisation. It is therefore necessary to tailor how information is passed along,depending on the person and the situation.

> *"Good communication skills! We are talking full brand communication. Someone who can listen, speak, write…"*

Two important sub-attributes of effective communication discussed as being important skills in an HR context were information transfer and persuasion skills.

Information transfer

At a general level of communication, HR employees are expected to be able to transfer required information across the organisation and amongst other staff. However, owing to the heterogeneous nature of an organisation, people working in HR are often expected to be able to adapt their style of communicating in order to be more effective.

> *"We expect people to alter how they communicate depending on the situation. If you are talking to the CEO then you may be more technical than if you are talking to administrative staff."*

> *"You [graduates] need to be able to cut your cloth accordingly, and tailor what you are saying".*

Persuasion

Additionally (though infrequently) HR staff are expected to provide clarity to a subject or a topic that is heading in a direction which may not be appropriate. Being able to influence a situation and to persuade people to make the right decisions are therefore important skills.

> *"So often you need to try to persuade the advisee to think that the idea you are giving them was theirs in the first place."*

POTENTIAL STRATEGIES – 3.Communication

- Develop partnerships between students and external organisations to practice networking and information transfer.
- Invite industry guest speakers from various Human Resource backgrounds to talk to the students. This provides various references to presentational skills, information transfer, and conveying information to an audience.
- Class support groups where students can meet and solve problems as a group.

- Use of role-play so that students can practice various aspects of communication from the viewpoint of different parties.
- International "buddying" system so that students can network, share information and practice language with other students from a foreign country.
- Negotiation courses so that students learn the science of persuasion and are therefore able to negotiate and persuade more effectively in their careers.

9.2.4 Strong work ethic

In the interviews, employers discussed at length the influence that experience has on the ability to perform; having complete dedication to the job was extremely important. Employers suggested that graduates needed to be realistic about their own ability and to understand that there was a large amount of information to be learnt, as well as being motivated enough to take on that challenge:

> *"Often graduates come across as if they know everything because they have done a dissertation...it is about understanding that everyone, including organisations, are different. They will need to shape and mould themselves to the organisation."*

Two main skills were seen as essential components of this strong work ethi: motivation and willingness to learn.

Motivation

Employers expected graduates to make up for their lack of experience by demonstrating a distinct motivation towards the job. Particularly important were high levels of enthusiasm. Additionally, graduates were expected to show that they had consciously moved into HR because they wanted to be challenged by the job.

> *"Having a sense of direction is important. We don't want people who have just fallen into HR!"*

> *"I expect them [graduates] to be full of enthusiasm...they have just set themselves up with all this knowledge and should be pretty hungry for the challenge."*

Willingness-to-learn

Whilst being motivated to take on new challenges, graduates were also expected to understand that they would need to continue their education. Employers wanted to employ individuals who were aware of how much they needed to learn if they wanted to excel in the post. People who showed the capacity to be reflexive were particularly valuable.

> *"With the changing world of business, it is entirely possible to run from one project to another. Actually taking time to reflect on what could have been done differently and to learn from it is really handy."*

> *"People who take on board what others say are going to be successful!"*

POTENTIAL STRATEGIES – 4.Work ethic

- Inspirational guest lectures to motivate students in their Human Resources career, giving both direction and purpose.
- Well defined course documents with clear learning outcomes. Online forums for students to contribute (e.g. blogs) will open up communication links between students and teachers keeping everyone engaged in the course.
- Work diaries to develop the skills inherent in working to tight targets and to self-motivate.

9.2.5 Commercial acumen

Understanding how a business functions in its own and wider environment was seen as important by employers. Being able to take small amounts of information from the industry as a whole helps employees to function effectively in their roles. Having an understanding of how an organisation works and ultimately an individual's place in it were seen as particularly salient. Consequently two sub-dimensions were perceived as critical: external knowledge and internal awareness.

External knowledge

Whilst the role of an HR professional centres largely on internal functions of an organisation, an awareness of how the wider business functions helps individuals to make better decisions and to give more effective advice.

> *"They [graduates] need to make the link; some sort of correlation between what they are doing and what is going on in the world of business."*

Internal awareness

Conversely, an awareness of how the business operates from the inside was also seen as extremely important. Graduates should be able to make the connection between the theory and practice of organisational function. Realistic understanding of where they fit in and where they can deliver benefits were similarly critical.

> *"We need to be there for every single individual, but more important-ly for the business. We need to know where we make a contribution to it."*

> *"It is very important that people understand the business function. You [graduates] have to be flexible enough to balance this with business need."*

POTENTIAL STRATEGIES – 5.Commercial acumen

- Use of up-to-date real life examples of developments within the Human Resources profession.
- Computer based decision making games simulating the business world.
- Short work experience placements within HR departments during vacation periods.
- Work based assignments/dissertations which require the student to immerse themselves into the organisation.
- Case stories using real life problems, where the students can then use the information to work towards a solution.

9.2.6 Team working

Whilst the majority of work conducted by HR employees is conducted on an individual basis it was felt that being part of the team plays an important role in improving how the job is completed. There were no sub-attributes of team working found during the interviews. Although less critical than a number of other skills, team working was, nevertheless, still regarded as a very important quality.

> *"A team player is essential. Whilst we do work individually, falling into a team ticks boxes."*

POTENTIAL STRATEGIES – 6.Team working

- Group based assignments for students to gain experience of working towards a goal within a team environment. Human resource substantive issues such as conflict resolution could be used as the focus of the project.
- Team based residential activities to build up team working skills.

9.3 HR Employability in China

Nine organisations in China which employed graduate students with HR qualifications were interviewed; including a university, research institutes, media companies, publishing and software organisations and social HR. As previously, directors or deputies of HR were interviewed for around

30 minutes and asked to discuss the most salient attributes they seek in potential employees. A process of ranking completed the questions and the analysis uncovered six key themes shown in Table 9.2 below:

Table 9.2 Classification of employability attributes desired by Chinese Human Diligence Resources employers

Dimensions of Employability Expected by China Employers	Sub-Dimensions (i.e. Attributes)
1. Desirable persona	a. Friendly and helpful b. Strong integrity c. Reliable d. Confident
2. Communication	a. Initiative communication b. Information transfer
3. Executive capability	a. Systemate working b. Problem solving c. Creativity
4. Professional knowledge	
5. Working enterprise	a. Working Diligence b. Working circumspectively c. Team working
6. Adaptive skills	a. Stress management b. Flexibility to change

9.3.1 Desirable persona

All of the HR managers interviewed shared a common view about the importance of an appropriate personality within the department. Having a strong sense of ethical behaviour alongside having the desirable characteristics of an HR employee were seen as critical, the sub-attributes summarise these HR characteristics.

"HR is a sort of job where people set standards and make judgements about other people. If a person has obvious ethical defects, he never can do things right by others."

"...staff here are expected to be embedded with clearer and higher moral principles than others. Only such staff can have a right position to tell others what is right."

Integrity

HR, as a people orientated department, is concerned with a graduate being able to demonstrate integrity; in short, those individuals who can critically assess (and balance) their desires, commitments, wishes, and goals. In definition managers used words such as 'honest' and'selfless'.

> *"Only people with integrity are suitable for a position in the HR department. In terms of integrity, it requires you to be honest not only to the boss but also to people in other divisions. You know, some kind of so-called clever people may try to lie. But nobody can be further cheated after one night."*

> *"...not only honest but being selfless is also important. I don't mean that you should only think for others - your benefit can't be taken from the loss of others."*

Reliable

Reliability was a key attribute identified by HR managers; specifically, the ability of potential employees to maintain the confidentiality of work matters.

> *"Information in HR work may usually be associated with the interests of somebody in the company such as personal information, income, job asse-ssments and so on. We like the [kind of] person who can forget the kinships and friend-ships when keeping those se-nsitive pieces of information. Otherwise, how can you trust him in carrying out everyday tasks?"*

Friendly and helpful

Linked to the previous attributes was the necessary demonstration by graduates of being able to show kindness, respect and assistance to others when required.

> *"All people have a psychological resistance to pressure. An iron personality makes people feel that they are being managed by the HR office. Being friendly and helpful allows your ideas to be accepted by people."*

Confident

HR staff experience elements of formal interaction with people from other departments. Graduates were therefore expected to have sufficient confidence in dealing with this formal interaction, especially with more senior staff members.

> *"HR employees should work on the behalf of the company, you know. In front of somebody you are the company and you are entitled the name of an organisation to talk with people, regardless of whether you are taking questions, publishing a decision or negotiating. A confident person can ensure that the two parties are in the right position."*

POTENTIAL STRATEGIES – 1.Desirable persona

- Role-play based on real industry situations and developed through team exercises in order to both develop working practice and to build confidence.
- Built into course material from the start of the programme should be elements which highlight fair play and independence of working. Students should be given significant individual tasks to build self-motivation.
- Opportunities to spend some time in a real-working environment, to integrate the theoretical knowledge gained and the practical application of it.

9.3.2 Effective communication

The second most important skill, as defined by the HR managers in these interviews, revolved around communicative skills. Human resource management is ultimately about human issues and therefore the majority of the work is related to collecting, exchanging and processing information about people.

> *"HR is about designing employees roles at work, looking for people to do the work, and keeping good people doing the work. All of it is about people. We actually need to understand people firstly and manage them afterwards. You see, getting to know people are really crucial… this is achieved mainly by talking."*

Initiative communication

Initiative communication referred to the fact that HR staff are expected to look for problems as well as solutions by initiating contact and communicating with people, rather than waiting for claims or complaints.

> *"HR is a sort of art of dealing with human interests and conflicts. If you don't want to meet and talk with people, how can you understand and find interests and conflicts?"*

Information Transfer

HR managers identified that staff are in positions closely related to both internal and external policies; HR departments therefore require staff that have high standards of written and oral communication.

> *"This workplace is a policy based department. When you talk or write you must do it clearly when it needs to be so, no more or no less than one word. Therefore, the words should very accurately hit the point. Hitting the point is crucial."*

"HR people may need to express themselves differently with different people. We say, words can be expressed in three angles and the artful one is the best."

POTENTIAL STRATEGIES – 2.Effective communication

- Information-sharing exercises – problem solving through information transfer practice.
- Oral as well as other format presentations should be integrated into assessment schedules; the ability to communicate evidence utilising a range of formats is essential to good communicative skills.
- Team sessions in which groups are given tasks that can only be solved using an approach geared towards co-operation. Roles can then be rotated so that students gain clearer insights.
- Specialist courses offered to all students on communication in presentation and written formats, these can integrate stories from highly successful industry experts.
- Non-verbal communication sessions, in which students aim to converse without the use of speech.

9.3.3 Executive ability

Important to HR managers was a graduate's ability to manage tasks effectively and logically, as well as working systematically; following practical plans whilst controlling standards and solving problems without being overly dependent on colleagues.

Systematic working skills

System-working skills require individuals to have clear working procedures when carrying out important tasks, including planning, executing, and controlling.

"I did get quite angry about a new member of staff who worked himself into a poor situation. Later he was fired. The work has been

given for a month and I really don't know why he didn't know that there should be a timetable to follow.

I really don't know why he didn't know that all those CVs should be sorted into different categories, and essential data should be put into a table before we have a formal meeting reviewing it."

Problem solving

Candidates for HR jobs were required to demonstrate a high level of independence when carrying out tasks or handling problems; the numerous unpredicted scenarios in each HR case called for a flexible but effective approach to managing a task.

"I get tired with teaching staff members about solving problems. If people can understand the basic concept, the logic and the process in doing things, they should solve similar problems automatically rather than being taught again and again like a nut brain."

Creativity in work

Creativity is integrated with the modern approach to HR working, centring on innovation in regulation, process and techniques in HR management.

"We want new staff who can undertake some new approaches by following the trend of social and business development closely, rather than following a routine that started ten years ago."

POTENTIAL STRATEGIES – 3.Executive ability

- Longer-term team working strategies such as business games enable team working to be developed using innovative strategies such as online interaction. These games develop problem solving and systematic working skills.
- Individual research projects which force a student to collate information from a wide range of sources and formats – enabling systematic and logical collation.
- HR situational puzzles to be solved in dedicated sessions with professional staff, to develop the real world problem solving required by employers.

9.3.4 Professional knowledge

Employers specified that graduates should have good levels of theoretical knowledge alongside legal and policy awareness. Systematic and rational thinking are central - basic theoretical knowledge is important in an HR environment – and a graduate who could carry out work in an innovative or difficult situation was highly sought after.

> *"When we talk about motivation, organisation structure and performance assessment, etc., employees with better theoretical knowledge are more confident. Although they sometimes try to use simple methods introduced from textbooks, we believe it is better than knowing nothing about it."*

Graduates also needed to have a good working knowledge of legal and policy issues, especially with regards to employment.

> *"Our daily work (HRM) is driven by state law and policy. For example[in 2008], the country issued the Labour Contract Law, which may dramatically increase our cost of hiring new labour and lead to many changes in our employment system... Now, many companies like us are attempting to solve this negative impact."*

POTENTIAL STRATEGIES – 4.Professional knowledge

- Multiple-choice testing frequently throughout modules, on the policies and procedures which have formed the syllabus.
- Applied and therefore longer written assessments which engage students in the linking of theory and practice through real-life scenarios.
- Interactive sessions with HR professionals and systems online in order to test and reinforce knowledge gained in a professional context.

9.3.5 Strong working enterprise

For the employers interviewed, a strong working enterprise indicated a purposeful or industrious implementation of work tasks and was further split into three sub-attributes: working diligently, working circumspectly and team working.

Working diligently

Working diligently was defined by HR managers as the ability to dedicate extra energy and time to their work.

> *"The work sometimes can be overwhelming and very urgent. I expect that my staff do not evade time consuming work, and do not postpone urgent work even if it may need them to contribute some of their spare time. There is an old saying: God helps those who are diligent."*

Working circumspectly

Communication of written information in HR is often highly detailed and candidates for HR jobs are required to work carefully on these details so that important information is not overlooked.

> *"Working on people related issues; we need people to be very careful in talking, writing, analysing and concluding, etc. Because the object of our work is people many issues can be very sensitive."*

Team working ability

Team working ability is embedded in the harmony of Chinese business culture. This culture requires informal communication, a friendly atmosphere, little conflict and an appropriate balance of people throughout the team.

> *"If there is internal trouble between members of the HR department, the story will be transmitted very quickly around the company. We certainly do not accept a graduate who has poor relationship building and coordinating skills."*

POTENTIAL STRATEGIES – 5.Strong working enterprise

- Outdoor, and possibly strenuous, activities integrated into learning schedules test a student's abilities under difficult circumstances.

- The keeping of a working journal throughout the module would demonstrate the inherent highs and lows of work orientated action.
- Extra-curricular activities such as clubs and societies would help engage students in greater team building exercises.
- Analysis of industry mistakes to aid in the identification, and implications, of small errors.

9.3.6 Adaptive skills

As detailed in previous chapters, the implications of the rise in single child families during a time of economic stability are workers who are unused to work fatigue and stress associated with times of greater hardship. This potential lack of tolerance for harder working conditions was raised by employers.

Stress management

To be successful as qualified HR professionals, graduates need to demonstrate an ability to manage both personal and professional pressure.

> *"Difficulties appear in work and life. The HR person needs to manage the issues of others, and should therefore be able to handle those difficulties better than a normal employee."*

Flexibility to change

Graduates were expected to be able to react to the evolving business environment effectively and efficiently.

> *"Some students are quite ambitious in planning a future. But they don't know how to connect their big future with their smaller new job. A big future cannot just drop down from heaven, right? If I meet an unrealistic graduate who applies [for a job], I certainly will not let him in."*

- Dedicated seminars and sessions examining the levels of stress undertaken in the workplace and strategies to manage these successfully.
- Examinations of key up to date literature sources for professional and academic knowledge in order that students are able to keep adapting to changing circumstances.
- Role-play techniques which integrate changing circumstances.
- Problem solving through group exercises.

9.4 Summary

The role of the Human Resources department in the success of organisations is well documented. The general goal of the HR team is to provide a supportive and stabilising role which includes building, developing and maintaining the human capital: employees. As such, HR professionals very rarely have the customer facing situations that marketing and finance workers do, it follows that the skills and capabilities expected are significantly different.

In both the UK and China it is clear that it is the personable skills of human resource candidates which are extremely important, therefore employability traits such as being confident, friendly and approachable are transferable between both countries. Similarly, having a good level of communication skill was also important in the UK and China; it also became evident that these skills can be taught via the university experience. Such a focus is understandable, since the HR role is as a communicator, negotiator and organiser. This status does not change considerably between the two countries. That is not to say that there are not marked differences, for example in the UK the highest ranked skills were 'project management' and 'time management'. It was evident that HR employees are expected to manage a number of different tasks at the same time. Conversely, these skills were not discussed by their Chinese counterparts. One hypothesis for this difference is the way in which graduates are "dropped in" to their roles in the UK; whereas in China they are given time to learn about their position before being given extra responsibility to work on a larger number of jobs.

Overall, there were some striking similarities between the UK and China that have not been found in either of the other two disciplines. There are a number of reasons for this, one of which being that the HR role is static in its nature and therefore easily transferrable to difficult contexts. Further assessment, outside the scope of this publication, would be needed to probe these hypotheses further.

SUM-UP

✓ HR professionals need to have a 'personable' nature.

✓ Confidence, friendliness and approachability are key skills in the UK and China.

✓ The HR role in the UK and China are fairly transferable, with only minor differences between what is expected of graduates.

Section C: Case Studies of Employability Enhancement across Disciplines and Continents

The case studies that are included in this section detail examples of current and innovative practice that could help inform the development of new programmes by other institutions and employers. The individual case studies represent some of the progressive work that is currently being undertaken which is helping to prepare graduates for an increasingly competitive employment market. The authors would like to thank all those who have contributed studies to this section for their support and willingness to share their insights and experiences.

10 Employability Led Course Design: the Development of the MSc Marketing Management and Strategy at Plymouth Business School

Kerryn Husk and Troy Heffernan
Plymouth University

Employability was at the forefront of the development of the MSc in Marketing and Strategy at Plymouth Business School. Effective marketing strategy is the central driving force in today's global business environment. There are wide ranging career opportunities for marketing strategy specialists and integrating these skills into a dedicated course implies values at the heart of the teaching syllabus including:

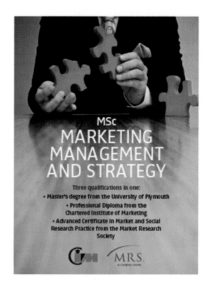

UNIVERSITY OF PLYMOUTH BUSINESS SCHOOL
www.plymouth.ac.uk

• Delivering advanced marketing management and marketing strategy theory in an innovative and creative way.

• Enhancing students' employability through integrating industry practice within the course structure.

• Developing educational outcomes across all learning styles to equip students with the knowledge and expertise to succeed in an international environment.

The programme currently incorporates teaching material alongside delivery by leading industry experts, as well as the ability to work with industry on active marketing projects. Marketing strategy is inherently cross (and multi) cultural, which is fundamentally built into the programme with the opportunity to engage in international field trips. The programme also encourages students to take both Chartered Institute of Marketing (CIM) and Market

Research Society (MRS) qualifications.

10.1 Employability

The MSc at Plymouth University was designed around students' enhancement of their employability within the field of marketing management. Throughout this book the theoretical and practical applications of employability theory have been outlined and, whilst these more traditional elements remain, there are a number of innovative elements which extend employment skills. Students enrolled receive the necessary specialist subject knowledge; however there is also a concentration in the delivery and assessment phases on more employment contextualised skills which are important to employers (Yorke, 2004).

Firstly, a module based around practice was incorporated whereby students have the opportunity to directly and critically engage with industry; students work on a suitably defined project with strong links to real-world practice. The module embeds work-related and work-based learning into the development of students and serves to engage individuals in the important visualisation of their own future (see Moreland, 2005).

It is this realistic invention of future situations which provides students with the desire to further their own development for a competitive workplace.

> *"Success will come to those who know themselves – their strengths and values, how they best perform, where they belong and what they should contribute; and to those who update and expand their expertise, knowledge and skills, who build and maintain networks, and who increase and display reputations."* (Opengart and Short, cited in Moreland, 2005: 17)

Secondly, an internationally situated module gives students the opportunity to undertake an international fieldtrip. This module revolves around the integration of skills designed to widen students' knowledge of international marketing theory; something which emerged clearly from earlier analysis of primary data in this book. Employability is an inherently complex issue, with no simple or set way of increasing graduates chances within the work market (Yorke, 2004). However breadth of knowledge is often specified and international elements are particularly useful for an internationally dependent discipline such as marketing. Indeed, according to the CIHE (CIHE, 2006), one of the key employability attributes of the business discipline as a whole is.

> *"[to] be self-aware, sensitive and open to the diversity of people, cultures, business and management issues." (Ibid: 51)*

These elements combined with a range of other strategies increase the level of employability of graduates from the programme and place the focus of course delivery firmly onto real-world applications of both generic and specialist knowledge.

10.2 Partnership with industry bodies

The MSc offered at Plymouth Business School maintains strong links with the two key professional bodies in the field: the Chartered Institute of Marketing (CIM) and the Market Research Society (MRS). This partnership gives students the opportunity to complete a Professional Diploma in Marketing from the CIM and an Advanced Certificate in Market and Social Research Practice (level 5) from the MRS. Such internationally recognised professional qualifications aid the future prospects of graduates by demonstrating the presence of key skills necessary for the workplace.

As well as this demonstration, the benefits to students of obtaining these professionally accredited qualifications are twofold:

1. Firstly, the declining status and currency value of higher educational qualifications through inflated numbers, alongside the need for

differentiation in an ever more competitive workplace, means that linked (but separate) qualifications (distinct from the degree itself) are beneficial;

2. Secondly, the strong links which these qualifications develop with the professional bodies in the discipline foster an integrated (and application focused) knowledge which would otherwise remain theoretical. In conjunction with the work-based and work-related learning delivered on the MSc, the real-world experience of graduates is significantly increased.

Central to increasing employability for graduates is the ability to be differentiated in a market where "the degree is not enough" (Tomlinson, 2008). Fundamental to the successful career path of a graduate is the ability to enhance the tools necessary in a real workplace (Holden, 2006), and the completion of extra-curricular qualifications recognised by industry bodies enables the MSc students to do just that. Graduates are then able to progress straight into industry with the knowledge that they have obtained a level of knowledge and applicability which will enable them to succeed.

10.3 Internationalisation

At Plymouth Business School, there is an emphasis on students' awareness of the global environment in which the sphere of marketing management exists. The literature in the field of marketing employability is wide ranging; however systematic meta-analyses conducted reveal a core set of 14 graduate characteristics which increase employability (Wellman, 2010a). Of these there are clearly strong links with the internationalisation of course material, including:

- Interpersonal relationships

- Networking and business relations

- Foreign language abilities

These are supplemented in Wellman's (2010a) lists by features such as knowledge of the global economy and business practices. Central to all of these lists is the notion that a graduate should have a holistic knowledge of how the marketing discipline sits within the wider business discipline and, more broadly still, the global economy. The integration of a module based around international fieldwork at Plymouth University brings these notions to the forefront and highlights to students the importance of widening their notions of the subject material. Importantly, the engagement with international elements also feeds into students' core and transferrable skill development enabling wider employability to be developed.

10.4 Further study, research and employment

Students who wish to continue in their studies are given the opportunity to do so; the successful completion of the MSc Marketing Management and Strategy allows students to be considered for direct entry into one of the faculty's doctoral programmes; for example the Doctor of Business Administration or the Doctor of Public Administration.

"The benefit of a variety of ongoing development opport-unities" (Raybould and Sheedy, 2005:261) cannot be under-estimated for graduates of any discipline, and for those in an area as fast developing and competitive as marketing are vital. In order to remain competitive graduates may often consider progressing through academic and industry research before entering the market completely; options which are fully integrated into the Plymouth MSc programme.

10.5 Structure

The programme was designed to provide candidates with a well-rounded postgraduate experience which places the emphasis directly onto employability. Students engage with substantive topics including marketing management, advertising, brand management, international and strategic marketing and marketing research. As stated previously, the programme also incorporates the opportunity to undertake two professional qualifications recognised by the CIM and MRS. Key to the overall experience of students is the interaction with industry and it is this direct interaction which is sought by employers. The involvement with live marketing projects gives students experience of matching their theoretical learning with practical experience; something identified by the preceding chapters as central to coherently integrated employability skills delivery.

The dissertation process also links directly with employability and conforms to the recommendations of Sweeney et al. (2009) in creatively situating assessments. From inception, three options were available to students:

1. The first is a traditional in-depth study of a particular area of theory of interest to the student;

2. Secondly there is an option to develop a new product marketing plan for a business idea or concept;

3. Thirdly, a consultancy option involving reporting findings from working with industry on a live marketing project.

Individual modules included in the programme were also selected and designed with employability at the core. This detailed structure is outlined in figure 10.1.

The issues outlined at the start of this chapter are reflected in the course specifics of the subjects a student would expect to engage with across key modules. For example:

• **International Marketing Management:** This is a 20 credit module with a European fieldtrip included. Students receive guest lectures as well as industrial site visits;on their return, students undertake further lectures and submit a reflective assessment linking theoretical concepts of International Marketing to their experiences.

• **Marketing in Practice:** This module involves groups of students going into local businesses and solving a range of marketing problems. They undertake research and deliver their findings and recommendations to the organisation.

Employability Led Course Design

MSc Marketing Management and Strategy

Subject Name	Credits		Timing	Staffing	Rational Uniqueness
PGBS0142 Marketing Management	10	1	September/early October	Dr Jasmine Williams	Introduction to marketing theory
MSR501 Social Research Design	10	2	Monday First 6 weeks of term	Prof Malcolm Williams	Insights into market research
Advertising, Brand Management and the Consumer	20	3	Mid October to early November	Dr Juliet Memery Dr John White	Develop creativity
International Marketing Management	20	4	Last 4 weeks of term	Dr Troy Heffernan Administration	International Fieldtrip Developing cultural understanding
Christmas Break					
PGBS0137 Contemporary Issues in Marketing	20	5	January to early Feb	Dr John White	Guest speakers Exploring cutting edge marketing trends
PGB0142 Competitive Marketing Strategy	20	6	February to early March	Dr Phil Megicks Dr Dulekha Kasturiratne	Developing strategic skills Strategic games
MSR525 Marketing Research, Methods and Practice	10	7	January to early March	Dr Jasmine Williams	Advanced research Complete the MRS integrated assignment
Marketing in Practice	10	8	Early March to April	Dr Troy Heffernan	Employability Working with local business
Marketing Dissertation Marketing Consultancy New Product Development Plan	60 60 60		After Easter until the end of August	All Marketing Staff All Marketing Staff	Academic Dissertation Employability Entrepreneurial skills
			Optional CIM & MRS courses		Professional qualifications

Figure 10.1 Programme Structure

- **The Marketing Dissertation process:** as outlined above.

Other modules reflecting the increasing breadth of delivery at Plymouth University focus on management and planning actions, research methodologies in market research and the links between advertising, branding and the consumer.

10.6 Summary

The MSc in Marketing Management and Strategy offered by the Plymouth University Business School incorporates employability skills into every level of the programme, modules, teaching and assessment. That marketing is a discipline which has a need for graduates with highly developed employability skills has been demonstrated in the preceding chapters and any postgraduate qualification necessarily recognises and integrates these comprehensively:

> *"...particular emphasis should be placed on developing and teaching not only theory but also facilitating its application, perhaps through the development of a practical toolbox of useful models and*

techniques. In addition we must recognise that the more general business, transferrable and employability skills and knowledge, at both the micro and macro-competence levels, are critical to success in practice and incorporate them into the syllabus and teaching. However, we must not "dumb-down", nor lose sight of the higher level cognitive and meta-competences so valued by employers and practitioners alike." (Wellman, 2010b: 130)

The increasing levels of specificity of these skills at various levels of education was outlined in chapter 3, and at the postgraduate level there must be a high level of dedicated, discipline specific skills which are recognised by employers as key to successful competition in the workplace. The MSc offered at Plymouth was built around these notions and the integration of other qualifications recognised by industry bodies as well as the opportunities to learn in conjunction with industry itself, means that graduates will be highly sought after in the workplace.

11

Knowledge Transfer in Higher Education: Enhancing Entrepreneurship, Employability and Global Citizenship in the 21st Century.

Lynne Hammond
London College of Fashion

This chapter is based on a working paper with the title: 'The strategic challenges of academic collaboration between UK and China in relationship to employability and creative curriculum.' This working paper forms part of the project: PMI2 China UK Collaborative Partnerships in Employability and Entrepreneurship for the Fashion Industries – London College of Fashion and Beijing Institute of Fashion and Technology.

11.1 Introduction

The rise of the creative industries and their importance to economic growth provides the context for this paper that attempts to explore China/UK curriculum approaches to employability and entrepreneurial practices for fashion design. The paper is based on the British Council Prime Ministers Initiative 2 Collaborative Partnerships Proposal for Employability and Entrepreneurship between two HE institutions. The University of Arts London; London College of Fashion (LCF) and Beijing Institute of Fashion and Technology (BIFT) are well-established institutions providing work-based learning for the fashion industries. Both H.E institutions have been working together on various projects for the last 4 years, and from these informal relationships a move towards a deeper collaborative partnership will emerge. The UN states that the creative industries already account for more than 7% of global GDP, with the UK employing around 2 million people and contributes to £11.4 billion to the UK balance of trade. As China begins to develop its creative industries and new knowledge economy, the emphasis is shifting towards the individual and consumerism. These trends are influencing the need to build creative capacity through education and higher level skills to impact on the strategic and operational levels of industry.

11.2 Key Challenges of the China/UK PMI2 Project

What are the strategic challenges for academic collaboration between China and UK in relation to employability and creative curriculum developments? The following two questions have informed our thinking and have provided the structure for this paper. The paper is an attempt to outline how, in year one of the project, we explored these issues to arrive at new learning experiences.

1. What infrastructures do we need to develop to strengthen our employability processes that enhance the students' awareness of international business environments in China and UK?

2. How can we develop better alignment between creative curriculum, professional practice and work based values?

11.2.1 Purpose

The project aims to demonstrate that H.E has an important role to play in identifying talent and adding value to the creative industries. The over-arching objective is to develop a curriculum and delivery methods that foster the skills and attributes which lead to graduates gaining and retaining work for global business environments. By exploring industry facing academic models and gathering industry insights from both cultural perspectives, this will lead to a curriculum that is aligned to professional practice and work place values.

> *"Advice and guidance provision and services to the creative industries workforce should be informed by the industry and incorporate industry input, sector intelligence, business skills and intellectual property awareness. This needs to be developed in a way that is innovative and relevant to the people and the industry they want to enter or move into".*DCMS. Creative Economy Programme. Work Foundation Draft Report, 2007.

The first year of the project consisted of three key phases:

1. The first phase has been investigating and exploring the current

Knowledge Transfer in Higher Education

employability practices in China and UK to map out similarities and differences.

2. The second phase has been the analysis of these data and information to identify the gaps, which in turn informed the writing of a curriculum project brief that is aligned to professional practice and global environments and staff development activities.

3. The third phase has been exploring the initial benefits of undertaking the project.

11.3 Phase One - Researching China/UK approaches

The research approach has been based on investigating two main areas:

1. Comparative mapping into employability practices in both institutions through the development of a tool to explore the employability activities/dimensions and project steering workshops with both UK/China academic teams to identify different approaches to how employability is implemented to students.

2. Three 'Company Interviews' have been undertaken to identify employability needs:
   - Company Visit 1 – Large Chinese brand supplying the international market place – LCF team visit 1 to China in April 2009
   - Company Visit 2 – Large Chinese brand serving the Chinese market – LCF team visit 1 to China in April 2009
   - Company Visit 3 – Large UK Brand Group serving the European/ Asian market – BIFT team visit 2 to London in September 2009

During the company visits, company representatives were asked a set of questions to identify employability requirements:

Question 1   *What does the company look for in a graduate?*
Question 2   *What is the recruitment process at the company?*
Question 3   *Do you recruit from Fashion Business courses?*
Question 4   *Have the company previously recruited students from the West?*

Question 5   Does the company manufacture in mainland China?
Question 6   Do you offer work placements
Question 7   Are there any graduate skills missing in the current market?
Question 8   What are the main differences between graduates from China and graduates from UK/Western countries?

11.3.1 Phase One Findings and analysis

LCF has a dedicated unit which is titled Fashion Business Resource Studio (FBRS). The FBRS model of employability is based on shared responsibility and dialogue between industry, institution and student to generate a mutually supportive enterprise culture linking education and emerging talent to industry practitioner networks.

BIFT has one career office dedicated to supporting employability with four career advisors. The careers team provides support for work placements, presentations to students on career development and has 40 relationships with companies for work experience. A set of employability and entrepreneurship activities have been outlined and used as tools to compare the differences in practices between BIFT and LCF (see table 11.1 overleaf).

Table 11.1   Comparative Employability/Entrepreneurship Mapping LCF/BIFT

Employability Activities	*LCF/UAL*	*BIFT*
1. Workshops to prepare students for work experience	Delivered to Y2 students By FBRS Power-points/One to one tutorials	Has a Career office with 4 people Deliver general presentations
2. Work Placements and Internships -	In Year 2 and Year 3 By FBRS Handbooks Industry database Students have a one to one meeting with specialist employability staff. One year paid placements and 3 month non paid placements	Students participate in work experience in summer Year 3 and BIFT has 40 relationships with companies – 2 months in length

Table 11.1 Continued

Employability Activities	LCF/UAL	BIFT
3. Industry Projects	In year 2 By FBRS with academics/industry Stimulated and Live Project Briefs	Strong relationship with companies who provide research information to students.
4. Showcasing to Industry	End of BA Course Exhibition of student work to industry	BIFT has end of year exhibitions and catwalk shows
5. Career workshops	Year third and fourth year students By FBRS/Power-points	BIFT holds graduate events and invite companies to come and meet students face to face
6. Alumni and networking	Website for alumni Networking events for alumni	Alumni network is established. Nearly 93% of graduates gets jobs – 5% set up their own business
Entrepreneurship ECCA		
7. Enterprise Centre	University service Free resources	Government supports business start-ups but Integrated within the UG curriculum
8. Enterprise weeks	University event Trade shows Information Packs for start ups	Lectures on legal problems and how to set up a business delivered by academic teams
9. Competitions	ECCA provide information on enterprise competitions	BIFT work with companies and offer individual companies consultancy
10. Funding opportunities for start ups	ECCA provide information on funding and mentoring schemes	Much easier to register a company in China
Enterprise Development LCF		
11. Fashion Incubators Support/Funding	Government funded support and University support for companies – studio/coaching	Beijing government
Global Citizenship Activities		

Table 11.1 Continued

Employability Activities	LCF/UAL	BIFT
12 International Projects/cultural workshops	International Staff and Student Exchanges Specialist unit for Flying Faculty to encourage student to integrate into new cultures Government funded projects for students to share knowledge and talent Specialist team for cultural workshops	BIFT staff are taking international PhD study, BIFT supports staff development programmes for international mobility and exchanges Students encourage to learn different cultures
13 Institutional Partnerships and Networks/Relationships	Has partnerships in approximately 30 countries	Has relationships with Japan, Italy, France and USA, Korea – both companies and institutions

Industrial insights

The company visits were undertaken during the first year of the project and have provided rich data and insights into employer requirements for future graduates, academic pedagogic approaches to creative design and employability support systems used by both educational institutions. Table 11.2 outlines the Chinese employability questions from two Chinese brands:

Table 11.2 Employability questions, China

		China 1	China 2
Q 1	What does the company look for in a graduate?	Grades, creativity, portfolio, technical skills	Creativity, business, skills, presentation skills, portfolio, work independently, has work experience
Q 2	What is the recruitment process at the company?	Company holds a recruitment assessment day and selects the best students. Selected students have a 3-6 month trial period.	Recruit all year round Through interview and portfolio which must show strong creative skills Sometimes set a brief at the interview stage
Q3	Do you recruit from Fashion Business courses?	Yes, recruit for communication and PR activities	At present, China does not offer specific fashion management courses

Table 11.2 Continued

		China 1	China 2
Q4	Have the company previously recruited students from the West?	Have employees trained in West, and returned to Beijing, however language is an issue	
Q5	Does the company manufacture in mainland China?	Manufacture across China	Manufacture across China
Q 6	Do you offer work placements	Offer internships during Year 3 for Design, Marketing 3-12 months	1-3 month internships
Q 7	Are there any graduate skills missing in the current market?	Limited specialist courses for this product group	Graduates need to have a technical awareness of how to construct a garment
Q 8	What are the main differences between graduates from China and graduates from UK/ Western countries	International students are very detailed and focused	Chinese students have a broader understanding of arts subjects, but less commercial insights, European students are perceived to have good attention to detail

UK Company Insights for Global Employability

Various meetings with a large UK fashion group have been held to discuss the company's vision and direction for the future. This has informed the project brief outcomes and activities, based on the company now wanting to open up retail spaces in China as well as strengthen their manufacturing strategies with Chinese suppliers.

11.4 Phase Two – Gap analysis and development of the project brief

The initial comparative research findings revealed the following:

1. There is limited inclusion of entrepreneurship inputs in undergraduate project briefs from both institutions;

2. There are limited resources to support students developing an understanding of international markets and consumers; in particular in China;

3. Chinese companies are looking for designers who have holistic skills, whereas UK companies are looking for designers who can be creative and trend led;

4. Project briefs are often developed in association with companies/ industry, but the development of international learning outcomes with global partners was new to both BIFT and LCF teams;

5. Both institutions had employability activities embedded into the student programmes and were delivered by specialist support teams;

6. Limited staff development planning was undertaken with regards to international collaboration and knowledge transfer.

Based on these six gaps identified, the teams included and developed the following inputs to support the successful delivery of student work, and they have also been used in the design of the student project.

1. Entrepreneurship Workshops
Workshops delivered in London and China – September 2009/April 2010

UK Workshops- To raise awareness of entrepreneurship education at LCF two workshops were delivered to BIFT staff. Two entrepreneurs who started their own companies immediately after graduating delivered the first workshop; and the second was delivered by an entrepreneur expert as part of her PhD project.

China Workshops – During the visit to China in April 2010 it was intended to deliver a workshop titled 'From Concepts to Concrete Business'. The workshop was delivered by specialist entrepreneurship experts and explored what it means to be a global entrepreneur in terms of values, branding, networking and project management. In addition, three podcasts on creative start-ups case studies have been translated into Chinese.

2. International Market and Consumer Intelligence Resources/Reading lists/ Staff Development

To ensure that students can undertake the research to inform their design ideas and prototypes a set of learning resources are being developed so that market information can be as up to date as possible for students to access. During the visits to UK and China time has been allocated to staff so they can undertake joint research trips into retail, consumer and cultural influences. Understanding how the Chinese consumer shops is key to effectively competing in this market, and knowing the apparel market in China will raise awareness of the potential of emerging growth markets.

3. Chinese /UK companies Requirements of Designers

What emerged from the company interviews was that Chinese companies are looking for holistic fashion designers that have a broad range of skills, but would place creativity over business/technical skills when they finally select a graduate. Chinese companies perceive UK graduates as having stronger attention to detail. All of the companies recruited designers on the quality of their portfolio; the logical order of the portfolio and presentation of the portfolio. Tasks that promote creativity have been integrated into the project brief.

4. International Project Briefs

Based on the company interviews and their business strategies for global growth the project was developed "New Global Opportunity – through community creativity". The project brief will be delivered to Year 2 undergraduate students during the Autumn Term in 2010. Students will work in groups and create a product range/capsule collection for the company brand that is growing opportunities in new and emerging markets. The students will upload their work to the university websites so that both UK and Chinese tutors can view the work, and also that the companies can monitor progress and developments. The final presentation will be through digital channels.

5. Global Citizenship

At the present time no workshops are being delivered to students on global citizenship as a specific topic. These areas will be discussed during the BIFT visit to LCF in September 2010; it is certainly an area which needs further development in order to identify the staff who can contribute.

6. Staff Development

During the visits, several workshops have been conducted to ensure that all staff have the necessary skills to deliver the projects. It is anticipated that Chinese staff will develop important learning resources for UK students, and vice versa for Chinese students.

11.5 Phase Three - Benefits

A set of benefits have been identified as a result of the China/UK academic collaborative project in year one:

1. International Work Placements/Internships

New international business networks have been developed as a result of the industry visits undertaken during the staff mobility activities to China and UK. The companies have initially expressed an interest in offering students from LCF and BIFT one-year paid work placements in either their London or in Beijing. This is a good example of how a UK-China industry/education network can strengthen employment opportunities for students who want to experience new global design challenges.

2. International Staff Development Activities

There have been numerous benefits to staff development as a result of the project so far, including opportunities for academic, employability and entrepreneurship staff to participate in international travel and to develop joint curriculum projects. The project has focused the team's thinking around the challenges of what are likely to be the significant skills needed by fashion graduates in order to operate globally, and to work in highly competitive and fast moving real-life situations.

3. Internationalising the Curriculum

The broader benefits of the collaboration are the deeper understanding of curriculum models, pedagogic approaches and knowledge transfer of UK and China Fashion education systems.

The project has drawn a diverse range of experts from both the college (LCF) and university wide (UAL): the Enterprise Centre for the Creative Arts (ECCA) – which is a centralised university service – has come to collaborate with LCF international development, employability and fashion specialist teams. This cross-cultivation of specialism has been required to develop new learning experiences. The project has required research and development into digital technologies to make the sharing of knowledge and visual materials appropriate for China and UK. In addition, the project has enhanced the academic team's knowledge of real-world challenges for the future of design and the role global communities in consumption.

11.6 Conclusions

The strategic challenges of academic collaboration between China and the UK have been complex, and three key areas have been identified as playing an important role in this successful collaboration:

1. Differences in Creative Curriculum Models – Staff Development Challenges

All of the companies interviewed indicated the need for strong creativity to drive product innovation. The research revealed that creativity is critical for all graduates to ensure a successful career in fashion; and the role of creativity in the fashion design process has been discussed during the two visits between staff. This dialogue has been important in understanding the differences in how fashion design is taught in the UK and in China. Through the development of the new project brief which outlines in detail the creative tasks and methodology needed to design future products, it is anticipated that this will be an important tool to raise awareness.

The competing challenges between creativity and commerciality have provided the context for developing student experiences that are based on these dimensions. Both Chinese and UK companies have been fully engaged to develop new learning experiences that introduce new global contexts, cultural differences and market challenges which open up to students new business models and consumer segments. Through researching and shaping new strategies for fashion design and product development, it is anticipated that the experiences will enable future graduates to seamlessly work across borders.

2. Differences in Employability Infrastructures – Engagement and Entrepreneurship Challenges

Both universities have strong industrial links and contacts that inform the institutional employability frameworks and activities. Both universities have also embedded employability into the curriculum to ensure that graduates understand the commercial needs of fashion businesses and to establish strong and lasting relationships with the industry. The engagement with companies in both countries is high and involves close interactions to ensure graduates are prepared for the world of work.

The impact of the project will be to directly influence the capabilities of students, staff and companies. The overall goals of the project are to improve the employment rates of future graduates in order to serve the international industries demands for highly creative professional staff who can work globally. The primary challenge faced is preparing students to be able to understand the strong cultural differences between China and UK, which must be built in the curriculum to raise greater insights into what to expect when working in this type of business environment. The language constraints are of particular significance and it is these needs which should be considered. Global employment opportunities will drive more confident, culturally aware and highly motivated students who can deal with global employment opportunities, and contributing to business growth through graduates' better understanding of the tensions between commercial and creative outputs.

3. Managing Collaborative Projects – Relationship Challenges

The management of collaboration projects are challenging, and require sensitivity to successfully build trust and long-term relationships with partners. However, the impact and benefits of undertaking such projects is important for future staff and student development. The need for regular communication with partners is critical for open and continuous involvement in the next stages. The need for management commitment and investment by both partners into such a collaborative project is great in terms of academic, marketing and support staff who work at the operational level. The relationship is also determined by the digital collaborative technologies that need to be put in place to build virtual and online meetings/projects, and how student's work can be viewed by all partners, with regards to e-design reviews, blogging platforms and the uploading of images, text and videos for sharing progress and outcomes.

12 Collaborative Development of an Online Module Concerning Employability and Entrepreneurship

Dave Burnapp
University of Northampton

This case study describes a joint project between the University of Northampton in the English Midlands and Shaoguan University in South China. This project was funded by the China Connect strand of PMI2 which is concerned with employability and entrepreneurship. The project aimed to create a jointly-validated training module for students in the UK and China to enable them to develop global entrepreneurship skills, cross-cultural awareness and communication skills. A core project team was created consisting of academic and careers advisory staff from both institutions, and further support was obtained from other departments of each institution, including e-learning developers and educational researchers when necessary. A specific and unusual aspect of the initial concept of this module is that it envisaged that the course participants must form collaborative online working groups consisting of students from the two institutions sharing materials and working together.

12.1 Overview

This project relates to several of the themes which are emerging concerning the internationalisation of higher education, including the growth of transnational education (TNE); growth of e-learning; growth of collaborative partnerships; emphasis both on internationalisation at home and internationalisation abroad; staff development; intercultural communication; institutional strategy; and the development of students as globalised citizens.

This case study will illustrate the steps taken to achieve the stated aims of the project, which were:

For the *students* to develop:

- Cross-cultural communication skills;
- Knowledge of the business environment of other countries;
- Entrepreneurship competences for the globalised world;
- The ability to work with partners of different cultures.

For the *project team members* to experience:

- Cross-cultural educational collaboration and development of new pedagogic skills;
- Interaction with students in different cultures.

For the *two universities* to achieve:

- Mutual collaboration;
- The development of employable and enterprising citizens;
- Networks concerning entrepreneurship with other universities, government and provincial agencies and employers in both China and the UK.

12.1.1 Background to the problem

There are many facets to this project, but the specific problem which this case study addresses is about the processes necessary for the development of *mutual* learning partnerships, which is a stated aspiration of PMI2 (British Council, n.d) and which was agreed by the project team at an early stage to be the keystone to the project's success. Put simply, even if elaborate teaching materials were written and an attractive and up-to-date virtual learning environment was produced, this in itself could not be a guarantee of success. If *any* aspects of the module were not considered suitable by *any* of the stakeholders concerned (including managers, students, and staff) for *any* reason at all (including different expectations of what form the learning activities should take, or lack of conviction concerning the suitability of the learning approaches incorporated into the course materials, or issues relating to acceptability and accessibility of social networking tools), then the materials simply would not be used and the ultimate aims of the project would not be achieved.

Hence it was decided early on that each stage of the project should involve initially researching differences of expectations and then having open discussions about any differences found, followed by jointly developing ways of bridging these differences, and piloting of the solutions which had been devised. The project team set out to seek ways to exploit the differences between expectations in the two settings in order to create a series of bridges to enable differences to be transformed into synergies.

12.1.2 Key learning points up front

- To take time to work through differences. Although the team benefitted from having bilingual members of the core team, and further benefitted by beginning the project with firm friendships between team members already in place, it was found that each step needed repeated clarification and an emerging ability to be able to appreciate the perspectives of other team members in other situations.

- To try to establish and share a complete vision of what the project is trying to achieve, and practice explaining this clearly and succinctly.

- It was essential to establish clear communication channels, not only considering technical aspects such as emailing, file sharing and online discussions but also to allow time for reflection and translation. This project, as well as having bilingual managers, was able to appoint a bilingual Chinese research assistant to ensure that opinions of stakeholders were accurately gathered to be incorporated into the emerging plan.

- It was essential to build bridges with other staff and departments within their own institution, as the project might be seen to be trespassing in areas of responsibility of other departments. To be successful it was necessary to recruit these as friends as, for example, issues such as validation will require their endorsement.

- It was essential to liaise with senior management at an early stage as any project of this nature will involve issues of resourcing. If possible, to get someone in a senior position to be a sponsor or champion of the vision. Project funding bids are likely, in any case, to require the signed endorsement of the head of the institution.

- The project team greatly benefitted from consulting a website concerning intercultural projects (Global People, 2010) which was itself developed as a result of a much larger collaboration of UK and Chinese universities. In particular the Life Cycle Model:' *a guide for those planning, managing or reviewing a project or partnership.*'

- To adopt as far as possible, and as far as the project funding body allows, a 'Sliding Planning Window' approach to project management. This is a recognition that overly strict adherence to an established plan will prevent a flexible response to changes, (opportunities as well as threats), which will always occur in any project.

12.1.3 Key issues

It has been shown in cross-cultural projects in any domain that a strict target-oriented approach, that is attempting to force through and impose the preferred solutions of any individual or of one party, is likely to jeopardise success no matter how expert this solution is. It is necessary to accommodate the expectations of all stakeholders involved to ensure success. What is described here, therefore, is the *process-oriented* approach which was taken, which involved all aspects of the collaboration and which, it is suggested, might offer lessons which can be transferrable to other collaborative educational projects. This case study will therefore record *how* the project was developed rather than details of *what* the project actually produced (for example details of the course materials which were developed, or detailed description of the technical aspects of the VLE which was created) as these details will be published in a suite of research articles concerning different aspects of the project including details of the course materials, issues concerning the development of the e-learning platforms and tools, issues concerning employability, and issues related to cross-cultural learning.

Some of the dimensions of the project which involved recognising and then reconciling differences include:

- as an example of transnational education (TNE), it was necessary to address differences in the two institutions' operations and strategies for example, relating to issues of validation and quality assurance;

- as an example of an initiative relating to employability, it was necessary to explore differences in expectations of employers in the two countries concerning employability competences, how these can be evidenced, and how institutions assist students in finding employment;

- as an example of collaborative course development, it was necessary to address differences in the expectations of teachers in the two cultures of learning concerning what they believe to be appropriate methods of learning, teaching, and assessment;

- as an example of a course involving cross-cultural communities of learners, it was necessary to address the differences in the students' expectations of learning materials and learning styles;

- as an example of e-learning, it was necessary to research the different experiences, skills and expectations of staff, (including academic staff and e-learning developers), concerning use of virtual learning environments (VLEs);

- as an example of collaborative learning involving students from two emerging and different communities of practice in relation to use of Web 2.0 applications, it involved researching differences in social networking applications in the two settings.

12.2 This case-study: what was done?

Before being able to submit a bid for funding, it was necessary to build a team which from the outset would possess the necessary competences for a successful project. This team-building stage, and the subsequent bid-writing stage, necessarily takes place before any funding is received, hence this is itself an entrepreneurial activity, because success, even for a well-prepared and well-written bid, cannot be assured and hence this involves a willingness to take risks. It is unlikely that institutions will be able to fund this form of speculative activity to any large extent in the form of remission from other duties; hence the first essential competence for project team members is a sharing of passion, a willingness to engage in these preparatory stages without any certainty that the project will actually come about.

In this case several fortuitous factors coincided to enable staff from the two institutions to share interests and hence rapidly to come to a shared vision of what a suitable project could achieve. It is important to note that the details of this project hence emerged from a top-down vision which then was broken down into the components and stages which would be necessary to realise the vision. The factors were:

- An existing relationship between the two institutions, including a Memorandum of Understanding, which had involved previous visits of staff in both directions. The two academics who became the lead managers of the project in the two institutions, both Chinese, had met on such a visit when a delegation of Shaoguan senior staff visited Northampton and had then established both friendship and a sharing of interests.

- The lead manager from Shaoguan University was already heavily involved in business planning competitions in Guangdong, which is a prime method of developing entrepreneurship skills in Chinese universities.

- There were existing movements of students from Shaoguan to Northampton, some as visiting students and some who were progressing onto top-up or Masters Degrees. Shaoguan academic staff, when visiting Northampton, kept in touch with these students and hence remained familiar with the academic practices there.

- Another Northampton academic who would become part of the team had visited Shaoguan several times and delivered short courses and lectures hence was familiar with the university and the academic practices there.

- This academic was simultaneously involved with activities run by East Midlands Universities International Careers Adviser Working Group, which is a coalition of Careers and Advisory services of the universities in the East Midlands, and had conducted research into employers' attitudes towards employability of international students and graduates, and as a result was keen to be involved with schemes to develop cross-cultural employability competences.

- The head of the careers service at the University of Northampton is a lead member of the East Midlands Universities International Careers Adviser Working Group, and was keen to find out more about employment practices in China, and how Chinese university careers services operate.

- Northampton Business School has an established reputation relating to the development of entrepreneurs, as well as a team of e-learning developers with experience in producing online materials to support training materials. Hence there was technical expertise to draw upon.

The vision which emerged during this initial stage of team building was for an online module which would involve students from the two universities working together in collaborative groups in a series of activities which would develop entrepreneurial skills and cross cultural awareness and communication. It was felt that this would necessarily be an online course, and that the medium of instruction and interaction would be in English.

The bid for funding included a detailed plan of the stages the project team intended to follow, and the following section of this case study will describe how this plan was implemented (and at times was amended) in order to produce such a course. The team found, in fact, that in some aspects the initial plan needed to be flexible so adopted a 'Sliding Planning Window' approach and asked permission of the funders to allow them more time to complete certain activities. This will be expanded upon later in this case study.

12.2.1 Activities undertaken and outputs in the first six months

Projects such as this will inevitably require the project team to involve other staff and departments within an institution, and indeed unless this is done at an early stage (and with a degree of diplomacy), the project team might be seen to be trespassing in areas of responsibility of others. Initially, the team needed to carry out internal consultation with other stakeholders including

Collaborative Development of an Online Module Concerning Employability and Entrepreneurship

students, senior managers and Careers Services within the two institutions. During this period, the existing channels and resources of enhancing employability and entrepreneurship within the two institutions were explored. The team also investigated the validation procedures and the existing Virtual Learning Environments within the two institutions.

Following this internal groundwork, during which there was frequent communication particularly between the lead managers, a project workshop to enable face-to-face communication was held in Shaoguan in June 2009. In preparation for this visit the Northampton team had spent a half day doing activities on the 'Global People Life Cycle Model', which is particularly useful for international projects with participants from different cultures. This provided them with guidance on the whole life cycle of an intercultural project from the planning stage through to completion and dissemination activities, and this helped to identify the core activities and the underpinning intercultural competences required at each stage of the project. This also allowed them to propose an agenda for activities during the forthcoming workshop in order to incorporate some of the critical features which have been identified earlier in this case study, including the following needs:

- To take time, for example for translation and reflection, rather than to impose solutions.
- To establish friendships via social activities.
- To seek mutual contributions and to welcome different perspectives.
- To allow breakout activities where the teams separated according to their speciality, e.g. to meet with employers, and to meet with the IT staff of the university.
- To meet and establish relationships with senior managers of the other university.

On the final day of the visit the project team reached agreement on the objectives of the project and its learning outcomes, identifying how cross-cultural skills and entrepreneurial competencies (which are linked to employability) could be combined as two intertwined key threads of the training materials and activities for students. They also reviewed and examined a number of key issues including: the VLE systems; the communication channels between project members; the project website; project dissemination in both countries; and the structure of the students' experiential activities. It would be easy to gloss this as a completely successful meeting of minds, but later when the two sides started to share proposed teaching materials it was found that there were still substantially different perspectives. To describe this briefly, the Chinese teachers were placing a greater emphasis on lengthy input materials for the students to read, whilst the UK teachers were placing a greater emphasis on application activities for the students to engage with. However, as a result of the working relationships which had been established during the visit, it was possible to merge these two approaches so as to produce materials acceptable to both sets of teachers.

Also during this period, several publicity activities were carried out, internally within the two institutions in teaching and learning publications and conferences, and externally by presenting at both the Association of Graduate Careers Advisers (AGCAS) Biennial Conference, submitting for the Annual ARG Awards, and close consultation with stakeholders including the East Midlands Development Agency and the East Midlands Universities International Careers Adviser Working Group in the UK, and the Research Society of Modern Management of Guangdong Province, the Research Society of Value Engineering of HEI in Guangdong Province, and the Marketing Administration Academy of Shaoguan in China.

12.2.2 Activities undertaken and outputs in the second six months

Following the workshop held in Shaoguan, the teams started to produce the module learning materials and tasks. This, as explained earlier, revealed that further discussion was necessary to align the expectations of staff from the two universities. Although this was easily resolved, the team began to realise that the initial timetable they had produced might require amending. When the team had written a substantial part of the course materials, the e-learning developers in Northampton converted a selection of these into e-learning objects so that piloting of the module could begin.

A second face-to-face workshop was held in early March with the Shaoguan team visiting Northampton. During this, the team carried out the first stage of piloting of the training modules which had been developed, and so achieved a deeper mutual understanding of important issues which would have significant impact on the delivery of the module including IT issues;

the structure of the training materials; and the level and types of material. The project team disseminated the project aims and activities when they met senior managers of the University of Northampton and other external stakeholders including East Midlands Development Agency, Career Services East Midlands Group, and Northamptonshire County Council.

A further issue which emerged during this period related to an aspect of e-learning which the project team had not initially envisaged. They had anticipated in their early plans that there might be issues concerning compatibility of the two universities' VLEs, but they had not anticipated a cultural issue relating to choice of social networking tools. Put simply (as this issue will be dealt with at more length in a research article on this topic) the team discovered that Chinese young people were using different social networking platforms than those mostly used by students in the UK:

> "There is a rapid growth and high rate of use of internet social networking in China: Godula et al. (2009) report that there are around 300 million internet users in China, with 200 million under 29. A key feature is the low usage of non-Chinese platforms such as Facebook compared with the dominance of Chinese platforms such as Bulletin Board Systems (BBS) which allows anonymous postings, Qzone which is aimed primarily at teenagers, Kaixin001 which added 30 million mostly white-collar users in one year, and Xiaonei which has around 40 million student users. Liu and Zoninsein (2007) state that 'a different kind of Internet culture is emerging in China - younger, more devoted, more addicted to speed and intimacy than its Western counterparts,' and also that 'Chinese also seem to be more likely than Americans to use the Web to share and form opinions'. Within education, Kang and Song (2007) report rapid growth leading to estimates of 10.54 million e-Learners in China for 2007." (Burnapp and Zhao 2009)

It was therefore recognised that it would be necessary to carry out further research in order to choose suitable social networking platforms to enable the interactivity on which the module was premised. The team believes strongly that academic interventions should, as outlined in 'The UK Professional Standards Framework for teaching and supporting learning in higher education', be based on research. Plans were therefore made to send an e-learning developer and a Chinese research assistant to Shaoguan to further explore this, and at the same time to carry out the second stage of piloting of the training materials and the VLE.

12.2.3 Future Plans

At the time of writing the team have secured funding for a second year during which the piloting and research carried out recently in China will be replicated with students in the UK, followed by a more in-depth stage of piloting which will use collaborative groups from the two institutions following a connected series of the module activities. Any amendments to content and to delivery platforms found necessary by this will then be incorporated into the final module which will then be made available throughout the H.E sector.

13 Using Summer Schools to Develop the Employability of PhD Students – a Case Study

Ulrike Hillemann and Elaine Walsh
Imperial College London

Employability of doctoral students has been a concern in the UK for the last decade, most prominently addressed in the Roberts Review of 2002. One of the main outcomes of the review was the realisation that UK PhD students had very good scientific skills but were often perceived as lacking in the area of "transferable skills". However, transferable skills such as team working, communication and leadership skills are of great importance to prospective employers. Students often might possess the relevant skills but were unable to articulate them or to develop them further.

13.1 Introduction

Only about one third of UK STEM (science, technology, engineering and mathematics) PhD students go into an academic career after their PhD (Vitae, 2009). However, many supervisors and students still solely focus on the academic aspects of the PhD and students are not necessarily aware of their broader career options afterwards.

At Imperial College, which predominantly produces science and engineering PhD students, a transferable skills programme was introduced to improve the students' ability to manage their PhD as well as the transition into employment afterwards. In 2007 it was decided to add an international component to the transferable skills programme, to enable students to develop "global skills".

International collaboration has become central to academic research and progression in academic careers demands a very high level of "international mobility" (Welch, 1997; Ackers, 2004). In non-academic careers, mobility is also often demanded; for example, a recent Association of Graduate Recruiters survey showed 44.3% of employers would like applicants to be willing to relocate (AGR, 2009).

However, whilst Britain is a popular destination for international students (there has recently been a 50% increase in full time international PhD students in the UK), British students are less keen to go abroad thus limiting their career opportunities. Erasmus data show 62% fewer UK students study abroad compared to German students (Erasmus TOTAL). This relative lack of mobility may limit UK students' success in increasingly global job markets.

The aim of Imperial College's "global skills" programme is twofold. On the one hand, it gives doctoral students the chance to get an international experience, to make contacts with doctoral students at partner universities, which can help them in their future careers. At the same time, these programmes have a specific focus on training in intercultural skills to provide the students not only with theoretical knowledge but also the possibility to reflect on their intercultural experiences in an active learning environment. Both aspects help the students to develop greater awareness of the global nature of their employment market as well as giving them an insight into the skills needed to be successful in this market. A central part of the College's "global skills" programme is the development of summer schools with our partners in different regions of the world, and where possible these are combined with an international research placement or a language course. The first international summer school was set up in 2007, together with partner universities from the IDEA League (TU Delft, ETH Zurich, RWTH Aachen, Paris Tech). It brought together 40 late stage PhD students, eight from each institution. In the following years the programme was extended to Asia, with a summer school in Singapore in collaboration with NUS and NTU as well as one in Hong Kong with HKU. These courses were designed for early stage PhD students and included a research placement at the partner institutions. The research placements proved very successful in giving the students a greater exposure to the host culture, as well as providing them with the possibility to make contacts for their future research careers.

In 2008 the Graduate Schools and the International Office decided that they wanted to add an international summer school for late-stage PhD students to this portfolio, which would support students by having a stronger focus on the next step after the PhD. This course would be designed to address the question of employability of PhD students as well encouraging them to consider entrepreneurial activity. Research and discussion with our

Chinese partners at Tsinghua University, Beijing highlighted that they too were considering how to better prepare their PhD students for employment. China's economic importance also meant that an exposure to Chinese culture and start-up companies would be both attractive and beneficial to British students considering an international career.

This case study outlines how this "employability and entrepreneurship" summer school was designed, describes the students' reactions to it, and then concludes with staff reflections upon it regarding what was learned and what would be done differently in the future. As such, it is hoped that it will make useful reading for others involved in similar activities.

13.2 Initial research

The planning for the joint summer school with Tsinghua University began in summer 2009, a year before it was to run. Having successfully bid for the British Council PMI2 funding the two main themes were Employability and Entrepreneurship, but there were many possible ways of addressing them. In particular, even though this programme was building upon considerable previous experience, there was no intention to simply "export" a British model of training to China; a mutually designed and executed programme was a key objective. Before making firm decisions about its design, a number of focus groups and informal interviews with both Chinese and British participants were carried out in order to gather views and information.

In China these involved about 25 doctoral students in total, normally in groups of six to eight. From these meetings a clearer insight was gained into their PhD experience, their perceptions of employability and how the PhD contributed to it. Discussions were conducted to gather their views about entrepreneurship and how this might be relevant to them and their careers. Contributions were requested concerning what they would find useful content in the proposed summer school. A number of academic staff and employers in China were also consulted, and they shared information about how they perceived PhD students and the sorts of skills they felt such students needed to develop to make a smooth and effective transition into non-academic workplaces (where desired) and also to increase their attractiveness to employers.

In the UK further discussions were carried out with doctoral students, both British and Chinese, but based in the UK. All of these early discussions were very useful when considering what to include in the summer school and the form it should take.

It was also very fortunate that our funding allowed three members of staff and two doctoral students from the partnering Chinese institution to make visits to the UK. These visits were extremely helpful in further developing mutual understanding with the Chinese partners. The two students attended some of Imperial's existing training courses for late-stage PhD students and were able to offer much valuable feedback upon them.

All of these initial data were used in the design of a questionnaire to probe more deeply into the issues of entrepreneurship and employability as they are relevant to PhD students in China and the UK. After piloting, this questionnaire was then distributed widely to PhD students at both of the institutions via their graduate schools. Its results further informed the summer school design. For example, it demonstrated some differences between British and Chinese students' views about entrepreneurship; the Chinese students had a broader understanding of the term and were more likely to view it as part of their future career path, perhaps hoping to start a business based on their technical research at some point. In contrast, the British students appeared to be less enthusiastic about entrepreneurship and so, since engaging them with this topic was one of the aims of the new summer school, we had to consider carefully how we would be able to achieve this.

13.3 Building on previous experience

Whilst it was important to mutually design something new for this summer school, nevertheless experience of running a two day course for mid to late stage PhD students at Imperial was extremely valuable. This course, called "Finish up Move on" (FUMO), had been running since 2006 and had won the national "Times Higher" award for *outstanding support for early career researchers* in 2008. This programme was designed to support students as they begin to consider the post-PhD transition. Running this course many times had confirmed the view that whilst UK PhD students represent a very highly skilled sector of the student body, they do face employability challenges. In particular, those hoping to pursue an academic career often do not fully appreciate either the very high level of competition for such posts or the relatively low probability that a post-doctoral position will result in a subsequent permanent academic post.

For those wishing to pursue non-academic careers, the importance of transferable skills is often under-estimated and a communication gap exists between students and prospective employers. The key lessons learnt from running this programme were firstly that the needs of the participants must be addressed in a time efficient way; late stage PhD students are very aware of time running out. Secondly, it is important to explain to participants the value and purpose of each element of the course; it is not safe to assume that participants will see the relevance for themselves. Thirdly, different topics were "bundled" in the course in order to reach the widest possible audience with crucial messages (including obvious topics such as "preparing for the Viva" with topics which, at face value, have less appeal such as entrepreneurship). Finally, involving PhD graduates (alumni if possible) in the course was found to be the best way to bring different career options alive.

In the end, a proportion of the FUMO contents were retained for the new summer school, whilst those topics that were too specific to the UK (or even to the institutional context) were dropped. New topics were chosen from the suggestions made by Tsinghua university staff, PhD students and employers during the initial scoping discussions and focus groups. The final topics to be included were therefore: preparing for the Viva exam; grant writing; carrying out collaborative research; team work; negotiation skills; leadership; self-awareness and values for career decision making; networking; interview skills; entrepreneurship and intercultural awareness.

With the topics settled upon, it was decided that the new summer school would be of five days duration. This had also been the case for the previous Asia-based international summer schools for early stage PhD students. There were two main learning points from running these five day courses that were applied to the new summer school design. Firstly, it is crucial to strike an appropriate balance between keeping the course participants busy (so that they feel the course is worthwhile and sufficiently challenging) and allowing enough free or more relaxed time for informal learning and networking to occur. Secondly, it is important to select guest speakers extremely carefully and to brief them thoroughly so that their input is coherent with the course's overall aims and style.

13.4 The "Grand Challenge"

It was critical for the success of the summer school to address the needs of both the British and Chinese students. The main challenge in doing this was how to deal with the topic of entrepreneurship. As has already been stated, survey data suggested that British PhD students may be less enthusiastic about entrepreneurship and less likely to appreciate it as a relevant topic compared to their Chinese counterparts.

To overcome this potential difficulty, the "Grand Challenge Exercise" was incorporated as a central and unifying thread throughout the course. This newly designed simulation exercise was built around an application for funding for both research and an entrepreneurial venture. The simulation focused on a situation many of the students might face at some part in their working lives, either in their academic career or in industry. Since the entire funding application had to be relevant to one of the "Global Challenges" (as identified by the EU, for example, ageing population, climate change, etc), it showed the students how their scientific research could link to entrepreneurial activity. It was felt that this would particularly assist the British-based participants to realise the value of the entrepreneurial activity. The "Grand Challenge" approach also highlighted to students the need to communicate the relevance of their research to wider societal issues.

For the simulation, the students were to be divided into eight sub-groups of five participants, each representing a fictional university in China or the UK. They then would have the task to form three larger consortia to apply for a fictional "UK-China Grant" to address one of the "Global Challenges". This reflected the increasing trend towards multi-institution collaborations for large-grant bids. Throughout the course, students would have time to work on their bids, focusing on both the academic and entrepreneurial aspects. All of the topics which were to be covered either through discussion of theory or by taking part in group exercises in other parts of the course needed to be put into practice during the course of this large Grand Challenge exercise. On the last day, the three consortia would present their projects to a jury of academic staff from Imperial College and Tsinghua University, which would choose one winning consortium. The competitive element of the challenge was designed to strengthen the motivation and engagement of the participants throughout the programme.

In addition to the strong business element of the competition, one afternoon during the programme was to be set aside for visits to small, entrepreneurial companies in Beijing and students were further encouraged to exchange information on the different conditions for research and entrepreneurship in the UK and China. Thus it was hoped that they would improve their understanding of business issues and in particular how researchers and businesses might interact.

Thus the summer school was designed with a dual structure, and the students were members of two different groups throughout. One was a role-playing group for the Grand Challenge simulation and one was the "home" group for the rest of the course. Within the home group, the participants would work together to digest the material provided as content in the course. In addition, as the Grand Challenge exercise was designed to be a challenging and intensive experience, in particular requiring fast and effective team work in an intercultural setting, the home group time was designed to help students to reflect upon and learn from their simulation experiences in a safer, less-pressurised environment.

13.5 The summer school and its impact

The five day summer school took place in 2010 in Beijing with 40 participants evenly divided between the two partner institutions. The post-course evaluation clearly showed that the course was greatly appreciated by those that took part. The value of the content was rated as high or very high by 92% of participants and 100% of them would recommend the course to other students.

Students reported having increased their cultural awareness. While one week is not enough for in-depth learning about a foreign culture, they had clearly gained much from having to work so closely in mixed teams, especially in the

Grand Challenge part of the course. Regarding the different cultures one UK participant said "realising possible misunderstandings was very interesting" and a Chinese participant said "I learnt lots about teamwork, and had good communication with my foreigner friends". Several students reported that the intercultural learning was the best outcome of the course and good friendships were made between Chinese and UK participants. Interestingly students from both countries admitted similar anxieties before the course; they feared that the other group of students might be more talented and hardworking than themselves, but discovered during the week that they had much common ground.

The course was also successful in addressing the key themes. Looking firstly at entrepreneurship, there was a high level of engagement throughout the course with the Grand Challenge exercise and good evidence of learning and changed attitudes to entrepreneurship in the participant feedback. All but one student strongly agreed that they had increased their understanding and knowledge of entrepreneurship. A UK participant said the course "has given me an insight into the business aspects within and beyond PhD research". A Chinese participant said:

> "...intense and valuable ... the Grand Challenge gives us the entrepreneurship experience".

The other major theme of employability was also successfully addressed. Only two students did not strongly agree or agree that their understanding of employability had increased. A UK student said:

> "...extremely useful since I have appreciated the important of developing multiple skills and knowledge".

a Chinese participant said:

> "...it helps me to think about my future career path".

13.6 Room for improvement?

So then, was the course a complete success? As always there were things to learn and things to be done differently next time. First of all, there are some general points to be borne in mind:

- Creating a truly mutual course design is difficult. Even with electronic means of communication, there is no substitute for face to face communication. Relationship building is of the highest importance in building trust between the partners. Assumptions of common understanding need to be clarified.
- It's important to try to understand the motivation of the different partners and to help all to meet their goals.
- It is necessary to be flexible about timings and deadlines and not necessarily to expect things to happen in advance very quickly. However a lot will happen when partners are actually together.
- It is always foolish to think you have got the cultural difference worked out.

Relating specifically to this course, the following observations were made:

- If at all possible the course should be residential for both parties, so that it is clear to all concerned that they have to focus on this very demanding course and will not be able to attend supervisor meetings etc. at the same time.
- Several guest lectures were included in the course – it would have been better to have these in the morning and have more active elements in the afternoon, to help to maintain the energy levels of the participants.
- It is important to try to create a level playing field for native and non-native English speakers. When this course is repeated, more task instructions in Chinese and even some in Chinese only will be included.
- Confidence in using their English was a crucial factor for the Chinese participants, so more suitable exercises should be built into the early parts of the programme to build up their confidence.
- The participants would have liked more feedback on their work as they went along, in particular regarding to the Grand Challenge exercise.
- It needs to be emphasised that the bids submitted for the Grand Challenge exercise do not have to be perfect – some students kept

very late hours on the final night of the course.

Both groups of participants worked very hard on the course, becoming caught up in the excitement of the competition. There were some particular benefits for each group. The UK based participants appeared to be quite inspired by the great enthusiasm of their Chinese counterparts, particularly for the entrepreneurial elements of the course. For the Chinese participants, the course was a great confidence builder, in particular that they could communicate and influence others using a foreign language. This outcome was very pleasing as time had been invested in a pre-course meeting with the UK participants, advising them to be sensitive to any language difficulties. This was also further discussed in the "home" groups throughout the course. Equal contributions from both groups of participants were further enabled because certain restrictions had been put in place to ensure the fair allocation of positions of responsibility in the consortia. This meant it was impossible for one group to dominate.

At the time of writing, a follow-up analysis is taking place which is gathering the views of all participants of the recent summer school programmes, to establish the sustained impacts of such programmes and to confirm anecdotal evidence of concrete outcomes. For example, several students have indicated informally that they are still in regular contact with colleagues met on summer schools and some are involved in on-going collaborative research projects. Analysis is still on-going, but the early results are encouraging, indicating a lasting benefit from attendance on such programmes.

Some elements of this course have now made their way back into the FUMO programme, for example aspects of the grand challenge are now incorporated in that course. An exercise looking at values for one's career was also modified. After discussing this with Chinese students, we added an item about making one's family proud and another about progression within an organisation which were not previously included.

13.7 Conclusion

The course described here had the aim of developing the global skills of STEM PhD students and in particular addressing their employability and entrepreneurial skills. Participants were able to take part in a challenging international experience. Encouragingly, all participants either agreed or strongly agreed that they were more likely to spend time abroad in their future careers as a result of attending this programme. An important objective was to develop their intercultural awareness. For example, one participant said that the best part of the course was "making friends! That's more important than any job you can find in the future". Whilst as the course designers, whole-hearted agreement with this statement is not possible; many references to enjoying working with those from different backgrounds provide good evidence of intercultural awareness having been achieved. This participant's comment seems to express the feeling of many who were involved in this project:

> "a very good simulation, a wonderful memory of working together with different people, different backgrounds".

The course used an experiential learning approach throughout to engage the participants and to make the learning memorable. Immediate post-course feedback demonstrated a clear positive impact on the students' perceptions of employability and understanding of entrepreneurship. Evidence gained from other similar courses suggests that such impacts are sustained (Alpay; Walsh, 2008). The current follow-up analysis is also finding evidence of sustained benefits. These include practical outcomes such as on-going research collaborations and attitudinal changes, such as being keener to work internationally in the future.

The summer school described here is a key part of Imperial College's "global skills" programme for doctoral students. It may be difficult for PhD students to find the time and the funding to take advantage of international opportunities during their degrees. However, the evidence suggests that even such relatively short experiences are valuable in better equipping participants for an increasingly globally competitive market place.

14

Entrepreneurship for the Creative and Media Arts - Nottingham Trent University School of Art and Design and Shanghai Institute of Visual Arts

Christine White, Professor of Narrative & Interactive Arts,
Alison Oddey, Senior Research Fellow,
Fan Xia, Vice Dean, Lu Ping Professor of Performance Design and
Sarah McNicoll, Operations Manager 'The Hive'.

Nottingham Trent University

Shanghai Institute of Visual Art

"To understand the process of creative genius, it is valid for business people to look at the model of the artist. The business of the artist is to create, navigate opportunity, explore possibility, and master creative breakthrough. We need to restore art, the creation of opportunity to business." (Brand week)

The process of creativity is fundamental to both art and business, and this chapter sets out to examine the key features of entrepreneurship in the arts in a consideration of the case study of Nottingham Trent University's relationship with the Shanghai Institute of Visual Arts. These key features are located in having a good idea and being able to sell it, being a self-starter with an interest in developing work from an initial idea to realisation. One of the key focuses for the project is for students who graduate to be able to form their own companies and to work together between the sites of Shanghai and Nottingham, creating e-connections for sharing work flow and processes.

14.1 Overview

Thus, a sense of collaborative working is integral to the project and as part of that process we have considered what ways of teaching employability and entrepreneurship are most effective, how it is utilised in creative contexts and creative businesses, and how in the context of the UK this process of working has a heritage in Art and Design practice. In China, the 'businesses' of art and design have not had a long heritage, nor has there been a tradition of Art and Design teaching at degree level. The purpose therefore is to explore the difference and similarities to obtain a position where we can help incubate these potentials and small companies.

In order to provide an overview we will embrace historical, educational and cultural perspectives, which all contribute to the background and context for the project. We will consider what both institutions have been doing, and where this sits in relation to the process of education. Further to this, we will examine some specific examples from our shared discourse and look at where this trajectory is taking us and the way forward into the future.

14.2 The teaching of cultural entrepreneurship

Most business practices related to entrepreneurship in the creative industries are linked to the craft of developing a product within the contexts of arts and culture. What determines an entrepreneur in any field, however, is their drive and passion for what they are doing. Whilst artists are generally passionate about their work they are not always able to turn this into a marketable sales or business opportunity, or to structure a total business which could employ others with artisan skills. With the changing employment prospects both in China and the UK, it seemed appropriate to explore both cultural differences as part of our project; and (if there were any) to the approaches of enabling undergraduates to embrace ways of making their art, crafts and cultural business into long term employment opportunities.

The project is now in its second year and much of what we have discovered has taken a long period of relationship building and trust, not that dissimilar to creating new networks in the UK or other western environments. We have relied on the Chinese for their linguistic abilities in English to be the way forward in communication, largely due to the lack of Mandarin speaking UK staff; however there are some staff beginning Mandarin, which has been seen in a very positive light by the staff and students of SIVA.

14.2.1 Exploring entrepreneurship in artistic surroundings, and exploring the start-up of new Shanghai-Nottingham companies

The project began from a concept of artistic entrepreneurship, which focuses on the artist as the main proponent of their own company. Distinct from many categories of employment and business, the artist is always a freelance creator of their own employment opportunities, and many are only employed based on previous commissions. Their own portfolio (and product overviews) of the types of work they undertake make the artist unique in their attempts to get, and sustain, employment. These practices have led to recognition of the artist as a creative force in their industry and to the popularity of creativity as a feature of business success.

In this chapter, we are using the term *artist* to encapsulate all creative practice that might be undertaken by students of Art and Design, so it includes new technologies and new media practice alongside manufacture, say, in terms of fashion and costume design, craft in terms of ceramics and glass as well as traditionally understood fine arts, painting and sculpture.

The need for creativity in business has also become more focused during the financial decline in the UK since 2008, where views about business models have been addressed and re-assessed for their potency and provenance. Added to this are other notions of sustainability, both in terms of an ecological agenda and also in the preservation of the business itself. The philosophy of a market and the proof of concept of such a market have also had to look at reflections of public perception of certain types of creative production. The predictability of consumer behaviour is also under review in this changing landscape.

Working in China towards developing these concepts is also quite challenging. Ideas of market and commercial activity in the UK in the creative industries have a long heritage. The teaching of art and design in schools (primary and secondary compulsory education) has been a natural development for children, something which was extended in the 19th Century in the UK with purpose built sites and buildings. These recognised a need to train a workforce in art, design and technologies for emergent creative industries. In Nottingham in the 1850s, this most clearly took the form of textiles and lace making skills but in other UK cities, this was extended to the relevant industries that were pertinent to the industries of the home cities, so Birmingham's Institute of Art and Design (1843 Birmingham Government school of Design) was built to support Birmingham's artists movement and then developed jewellery and architecture specialisms. Manchester College of Art and Design (1881) and Leeds School of Art were involved in similar developments as Municipal investments in the training in the Arts, (now Manchester Metropolitan and Leeds College of Art (1846), respectively).

This heritage is indicative of the way in which Art & Design developed as a natural partner to business and industry with a clear political policy during the 19th century. In the UK this has been further enhanced by the way in which these schools of learning were brought under the jurisdiction of the polytechnics, established centres of excellence which trained and specifically developed skills in the individual which directly related what they learnt to the industry that would employ them.

In the 21st century ideas of skills training at a high level are again in the ascendancy. Recognition of the need to pass on skills and crafts, but also to develop the individual's ability to use new technologies (both digital and analogue), and to gain skills in new approaches to production and business, have all served to change the way in which key knowledge in Art & Design has innovated.

Further developments in the Art and Design curriculum for schools, foundation and now A-level have all had a particularity of training which reflects sector skills councils such as Skillset and produce specific results. Foundation has for many years been the mainstay of recruitment into tertiary level and degree-qualification study in Art and Design. The costs and additional years of study have not only collapsed this process and altered the nature of the student (and their perceptions of the work they may do), but has also changed the understanding of the worth and value of such study.

The PMI programme has given us the chance to review some of these aspects as part of research geared towards developing employability and entrepreneurship within the Art and Design curriculum; and to question what we teach in this context and why. This has been of particular relevance when working with our Shanghai partner, the Shanghai Institute of Visual Arts. In order to further consider these developments it is worth, at this stage, outlining where the history of Art and Design training lies within the Chinese education system, as it is within this context that similarities in perceptions and differences in process can be reviewed.

14.2.2 History of art and design training in China

The various kinds of visual arts in China have developed under the direct patronage of different imperial dynasties. The modern democratic communist China has the following categories of visual arts:

- Calligraphy
- Painting
- Sculpture
- Pottery
- Architecture
- Bronze casting
- Jewellery
- Photography
- Cinema

The last two art forms have been recent developments; however, the other forms have survived in the history of Chinese art under imperial patronage. The main patrons of each art form are listed below:

- Calligraphy – Xia Dynasty and Jin Dynasty
- Painting – all dynasties
- Sculpture – Qin Dynasty
- Pottery – Han Dynasty
- Architecture - Qin Dynasty
- Bronze casting – Xia Dynasty and Song Dynasty
- Jewellery - all dynasties

The history of Chinese art has a prominent part to play in Chinese history as *the indicator of the quality of life* of the Chinese people. Certain art forms like calligraphy have required specialised training and careful practice, a pastime that could only be afforded by a select few in the nobility; while others like sculpture, pottery, architecture, jewellery, have been a professional undertaking. This heritage has been indevelopment since 1977, when individuals were able to apply for university for the first time after the Cultural Revolution. Some of the masters teaching in universities in China have staff who were part of the group which had this opportunity. The teaching, though, followed the pattern of master artists and crafts-people sharing skills and knowledge with their pupils through working in their studios and so was very prescriptive. Shanghai Institute of Visual Arts, which is part of Fudan University, was established in 2005 and set out to follow a western pattern of Art & Design education, though they also have visiting lecturers and professors who run studios.

Recognition of the need to be acquainted with new technologies and to have a sense of market is part of current Chinese training. This is, in part, to do with the job market in certain industries; for example, China has a vibrant film, television and animation industry with a need for live performance design and exhibition design.

In this study, creative and media industries such as performance, entertainment, television design and production, film, animation and games are the foci. However we also allude to Fine Art practice in the UK, around establishing new businesses for graduates. In a recent visit to Beijing, we were taken on a tour of student work in a makeshift gallery, where students 'picked up' interested tourists to show their work. The class teacher was back at the gallery and the students examined their tutors', their own and their colleagues' work, usually depicting traditional calligraphy skills or classic scenes painted on silk with the aim of getting the tourist to buy. This was then added to the assessment of work which the student received. The more an individual sold, the more one demonstrated an entrepreneurial ability. This may be anathema to western understanding of encouraging entrepreneurship, but it certainly makes students recognise that their work has to be commercially viable.

The Chinese economy is the second largest globally and has rapidly become a major force in the world's digital economy, where it is now the leading producer of colour TVs, cell phones, desktop PCs and DVD players; with the industry poised to dominate in the manufacture of high-end digital products. The Chinese government is aware that prosperity based on manufacturing has a limited lifespan and is now looking to encourage the development of a knowledge-based economy. Alongside this, China has the largest number of mobile phone users globally with more than 850 million mobile-phone users

(62.8% of the population). There are over 420 million internet users in China, mostly using Baidu.com as their main search engine. The speed of this digital network expansion has created a massive demand for well-designed and delivered content that the industry is struggling to cope with.

Beijing aims to convert to digital TV faster than in the U.S and Europe, which will make China a crucial test market for new digital technologies. Subsidies to media outlets have been cut and this has caused heavy competition between newspapers, radio talk shows and television programmes to engage their audience by improving the style and the design of their content. There is a real and urgent demand for skilled digital designers, technicians and innovators to provide engaging content for consumers. In order to supply the workforce for the estimated growth in digital media outlets, vocational programmes must be formulated and delivered to meet the needs of the industry.

Design programmes in the UK ascribe to the notion that modern graduates need to be inventive, creative, communicative team orientated problem solvers who challenge concepts, develop new theories and are able to think 'outside the box'. These are the type of graduates that the university sector in China is being vigorously challenged by the government to develop. The Chinese Ministry of Education has mandated the Chinese Service Centre for Scholarly Exchange to work in collaboration with a number of key universities to develop "vocationally relevant" education. The key vehicle it has identified for achieving this is the British Foundation Degree.

Usually in China, children at the age of 6 begin to learn in formal schools, as shown in the diagram above. Preliminary schools are graded from 1 to 6 and children will therefore spend 6 years in these schools. Students then take an exam held by an educational government in their local area. After finishing this exam, students will undertake another 3 years in junior school, also examined by the educational government. Subsequently, students intending to study in university will attend a senior school for 3 years; whilst students intending to work will attend a vocational school for 4 or 5 years.

Students choosing senior school will take an examination held by the state; if they complete it successfully, they will have the opportunity to go to university and continue to study for 3 or 4 years. Those students studying at University for 3 years will be awarded a diploma, whilst 4 years constitutes a degree. Students attending a vocational school will also have access to opportunities to study in university, and subsequently to obtain a diploma or degree.

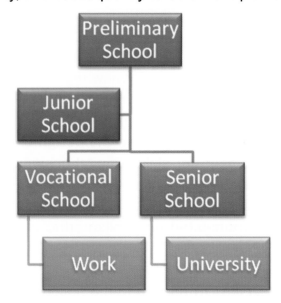

Figure 14.1 The education system in China

Unemployment in both countries is set to rise if ways to develop students who can create new business opportunities are not found; much of what has been researched relates to an ambition gap. Whilst, in the UK, 50% of the population want to start their own business only 5.8% actually do. The potential for creating a 'silicon roundabout' in the East-End of London (near the site of the Olympic village) is intended to help the high-tech development in the UK. There is some dispute as to whether the UK can compete in this market to the same extent as Silicon Valley in the USA, which pulls in venture capital funding of around $4.8 million (as opposed to David Cameron's assessment for London as being £200 million).

"A raft of other measures was also announced to improve the climate for technology and entrepreneurialism in the UK. These include an Entrepreneur Visa to enable people with good business ideas and financial backing to set up their business in the UK, and an independent six-month review of the Intellectual Property framework. UK Trade & Investment will also establish a presence in East London." (Source: http://www.number10.gov.uk/news/topstorynews/2010/11/pm-announces-east-london-tech-city-56606).

Global Entrepreneurship week and research from Enterprise UK suggests that a self-employment rate of 1% would boost GDP in the UK to around 1.5% and add £22bn to the economy. Therefore, encouraging these ways of thinking is a vital part of the argument for supporting training in art and design subjects in both countries, the discipline is also therefore inherently political.

Teaching entrepreneurship clearly has its challenges, not least of which is creating the right culture for ideas in the first place, which then can develop into the process by which companies achieve start-up status and funding; namely a unique selling point, a genuine brand, a sincere marketing story, a quality product, innovation and ambition. Both SIVA and Art & Design NTU have techniques for offering ways to inspire and achieve these links between learning and industry. These include student competitions, briefs sets by industry and existing companies, work placement and work experience. However some of the more productive developments have been in the area of incubator training; that is, 'time-out' to test the idea of being an entrepreneur.

14.2.3 Knowledge transfer: being entrepreneurial

As part of the sharing project with SIVA we identified what both institutions already did and which we felt contributed to making students entrepreneurial. These are detailed below in both tabular and listed formats:

- Competitions – usually with industrial partners which set briefs which are real and have a relevance to the company business and their development for the winning students. This might be in the form of a commission for work from the project, or a future contract for work based on the skills demonstrated through the competitions.

- Placements & Work Experience – these are short unpaid engagements and can vary from 2 days(particularly on film shoots) or for up to ten weeks. These kinds of placements have to have this range of flexibility based on the variety of activities within the industries that can be accommodated.

- Study Abroad & Erasmus Exchange – where students have opportunities to learn from other courses and practices, engaging with different cultures and industries.

Table 14.1 Art and Design in Nottingham

	Guide Title	Description
Employer facing guides	"Introduction to Sandwich Work Placements"	Overview of the sandwich placement process and the benefits of sandwich placements.
	"Guide to Sandwich Work Placements"	Provides more detailed information about how to arrange and deliver a sandwich placement.
Student facing guides	"Your Guide to the Benefits of a Sandwich Placement Year"	Overview of the sandwich placement process and the benefits of doing a sandwich placement year.
	"Your Guide to Getting a Sandwich Work Placement"	Provides students with information about applying for placements and preparing for placement recruitment.
	"Your Guide to Overseas Sandwich Work Placements"	Provides students with an overview of factors to be considered when choosing or preparing for an overseas placement.
	"Your Guide to Going on Placement"	Provides information to help students prepare for their placement and to give an overview of the placement year, including requirements.

- Skillset – Nottingham Skillset Media Academy, which covers our media courses, has links directly into media companies in the region and nationally. These courses have been accredited as having relevance to business and industry. We also have a Foundation in Arts Media Creatives programme which has employment and work with a small company embedded as part of the study.

- Fine Art Entrepreneurship - Initiatives for start-ups in Fine Arts have been developed through Professor Terry Shave, who has developed a number of off-site galleries for graduate artists. Some examples of these are 'Tether' and 'Moot'.

Tether was formed in 2007 by a mixture of visual artists who graduated from Nottingham Trent University plus practitioners from other backgrounds. The group was founded out of a desire to stay in Nottingham and maintain the work ethic and sense of community that formed whilst studying at university. Tether Studios consists of two galleries, The Wasp Room and Max Warburg Space, a social space with a screen for curated video works; The Black Swan, a disco-themed water closet and an event/lecture space, Tethervision Studio. The group also operates as a collective, producing collaborative installations and video works, as well as curating an online archive for video art and videos about art, Tethervision.

Another artist initiative along the same lines is Moot. Moot opened its doors in October 2005 in the Sneinton area of Nottingham as an artist-led project space. It set out with an outward looking perspective by working with artists from all over the country and abroad. Its programme is a combination of solo and group exhibitions, off-site activities and publication projects. Moot does not formally represent artists; the gallery takes part in art fairs including the Zoo Art Fair to assist artists in establishing relationships with collectors and curators. A not-for-profit organisation, Moot receives public funding and operates commercial activity to fund its programme. In September 2008, the gallery moved to a new premises taking over the ground floor of a four storey Victorian warehouse. Working alongside the studio group Stand Assembly, the three floors above the gallery have been transformed into artists' studios and a project space for 20 artists and curators.

14.2.4 Art and Design in Shanghai

- College Enterprise Cooperation – this involves staff leading projects with companies. Some companies involved include: Jahwa Joint Stock Company, packaging and branding company, Shanghai Aurora, Esko Trading Company Shanghai, Jielong Industry Group Co., Ltd. Shanghai.

- Other company involvements include the Shanghai Modern Architectural Design & Research Institute Co., Ltd; China Business Printing Group; Performance Training Base in Guangzhou; lighting design Laford Photoacoustic Science and Technology Co., Ltd.; Shanghai Technical Service Centre performance space design; Creative Park Triangle and M50.

14.2.5 Public engagements and commissions

This area deals with outside commissions which may be led by a member of staff, but which students produce work for. These are just a sample of the types of activities:

Chinese porcelain gift packaging design 2010, Shanghai Art Fair Culture and Art Development Co., Ltd; Yangzhou fireworks in March, Economic and Tourism Festival opening ceremony of the event planning marketing plan 2010, Commodities Co., Ltd; Information age 2009, World Expo Group, the Expo Center; Memory – Fly, 2009, World Expo Group, the Expo Center; Student Art Exhibition 2010 Shanghai Carrefour; Creative Industry Forum 2010 in Hong Kong Chinese Cultural Centre of Contemporary Photo; Landscape Architecture in Shanghai, roof space from the Shanghai Education Commission 2009; 2009 Siemens OSRAM LED lamps Creative Design Contest 2009; 2009 Bosideng International Building Image Design Competition 2009, Investment and Development Co., Ltd. from Shanghai; CNN Center in Yangpu District Yangpu District, 2009, cable television; Metro model of the design today Huai'an 2009 and Hebei TV News Center Transformation Design 2009.

14.2.6 Studio based projects

This work is packed with practical projects designed to simulate the combination of the project, and demand to see the latest packaging materials, the development and use of technology, as well as highlighting the practical ability of students and market adaptability.

- Product Design Studio: In all types of product design and development.

- Environmental Art Design Studio: In all types of indoor and outdoor environmental art design and engineering.

- Business Planning Workshop: The studio is mainly engaged in creative, planning, brand management, project management and advertising design.

- Integrated Design Studio: The studio emphasises the concept of contemporary design and art between the penetration and integration, focusing on cross-border inter-disciplinary field of design, encouraging students to absorb the forefront of comprehensive knowledge of art and ideas, and skills in the use of language skills, the pursuit of design originality.

- Visual Communication Design Studio: The studio is mainly engaged in advertising design, web design, (CI) corporate image design, visual communication that focuses on training students to understand the latest achievements and development trends, to grasp the strong graphic design and operational management capabilities.

- Landscape Design Studio: Engaged in various public facilities, landscape sketches, tourism project development, and design of residential quarters.

- Brand System Planning and Design Studio: Engaged in various enterprises, sports, business, brand planning and design of the system.

- Art and design studio performance space: Engaged in various films, theatre, sports and performing arts space design business.

- Exhibition Planning and Design Studio: In all types of professional exhibition and business activities in the planning and design.

14.2.7 Awards and competitions

- "Challenge IT - " Intel's Cup "Design Innovation Competition 2006" by Intel Corporation and Shanghai Fudan University, co-sponsored by School of Visual Arts, designed to provide college students can display their talents into full play and creativity, the theme of practice through academic competition, leading to research and development, into the industry, while promoting the development of advanced manufacturing and modern services creative advance. The mission is to explore and promote the production, study and research combined with the reform of higher education in art and design, training and the introduction of digital technology combined with the art of living for a new generation.

- To meet the 2010 Shanghai Expo, Multi-dimensional interpretation of the conception of Better City, Better Life, Utopia Realisable-Exhibition of Yona Friedman was held by O Art Center of Shanghai Institute of Visual Art, together with the Bund 18 at Bund 18 Creative Center (29th April 2007 – 16th May 2007).

- 2010 Shanghai Art Exhibition, our hospital two designs - Expo Theme Pavilion, the Chinese Museum planning report and with the change in the country. Exhibition had more than 600 works, nominated for 35 awards.

- SIVA students were short-listed in the 2010 8th International Design against Fur Poster Competition.

- Chen Xiaowen, student from College of Design, won the second prize in the 8th International Design against Fur Poster Competition (China).

- DAF Eighth International University in 2010 against the Fur, Art International Design Competition Finalist Rabbit Revenge.

- Excellent commercial image of 2010 Shanghai Design Competition Award of Excellence Oriental charm Shanghai (Yu Yuan Li Celeste Court).

- 2010 "One Show Advertising Design Competition" National Excellence Award Come go with me Group Min Jie Min Jiang.

- 2010 Student Home Design Competition, Shanghai "Tomorrow Design Star" Outstanding Organization Award winner Chen Yuehao.

- M50 creative cutting-edge National Design Competition 2009 Award nomination spring ShanghART shelves.

- Third National Student Advertising Competition 2009, the Ministry of Education Artistic Excellence Award.

- Third National College Advertising Art Contest (Shanghai Division) first prize of Shanghai Education Committee to enjoy the moment belongs to us.

- 2008 First sofapop Fashion Design Competition Shanghai dozen awards.

- And finally, in order to improve the visibility of SIVA, and to promote the communication between the students within the college, and between subject disciplines in the different areas, SIVA and society, to improve the enthusiasm of the students, and promote the creativity of students; to provide students with a platform for well-known designers to work with and create an active atmosphere at SIVA while exploiting the student's creativity and practical ability, SIVA hosted the "Open Week" activities where the students could sell their skills and products that they had made.

In addition to this, SIVA has an employer fair each year where employers are paid to attend and to meet with students, who themselves have prepared their CV and often get work as part of the day's events. Students also go through relevant interviews with these companies.

14.2.8 Shanghai Nottingham business landscape

Shanghai Media & Entertainment Group (SMEG) is one of the largest media conglomerates in China. Founded on April 19, 2001, SMEG is a major media content provider in China that also manages other culture-related businesses such as performances, exhibitions, tourism and hotels. The company comprises nine subsidiaries:

Shanghai Media Group (radio stations in Shanghai); Shanghai Film Group (film, animation, documentary productions in Shanghai); Oriental Pearl (Group) Co., Ltd.; SMEG Performing Arts Centre; SMEG Special Events Office; SME Industry Co., Ltd.; SME Technology Development Co., Ltd.; STR International Holdings Co., Ltd.; Shanghai Film Archives.

Whilst all the studios are located in Shanghai, they do not all function within the same facility; a number of studios have gone through different name changes throughout the years.

Also in the M50 district of Shanghai is the Camera Movie and Television Media Corporation. M50 is the complex that has become the Moganshan Road, Art District in Shanghai, formerly a set of dilapidated warehouses the complex, just south of Shanghai's Suzhou Creek, has been turned into the premier location for Shanghai's modern art movement. There are all kinds of galleries displaying everything from what have become much-copied black and white portraits of Shanghai's urban development, to sculpture and bizarre statuary made from scrap metal. The site attracts many tourists and has developed into a cultural area for the city.

Shanghai Oriental Pearl (Group) Co., Ltd. (OPG) is the first cultural company to be floated on the stock market and has 23 subsidiary companies. Its recent major businesses include touring, radio and TV transmission services, media investments & advertising operation and real estate investment. OPG strategically sets touring as their basis and media as a primary goal and has been listed as one of the 50 most pivotal large-scale enterprises by Shanghai government, and one of the 50 most influential listed companies in the Chinese stock market.

The Oriental Pearl Radio & TV Tower, one of OPG's subsidiaries, is the tallest Radio & TV towers in Asia and the 3rd tallest in the world. At a height of 468m the tower is now the most recognisable landmark in Shanghai. The Shanghai International Convention Centre includes a five-star hotel, various multi-function meeting-rooms and a large-scale banqueting-hall. The Oriental Pearl Transmission Co., Ltd. has undertaken wireless broadcasting and TV signal and data transmission services in the Shanghai area. Besides its continuous transmission of TV programmes to millions of families in Shanghai and East China, it has also developed added-value business. "Oriental Greenland" Management Centre is one successful example of OPG's outputs and has taken on the operation of the Shanghai Youth Off-Campus Activity Centre; covering an area about 5 600 mu, this centre is an important comprehensive site combining off-campus education, sightseeing, recreation and entertainment. OPG has also invested a lot of money in the construction of university students' apartments for the Shanghai Songjiang University City, setting an important precedent for education investment.

OPG developed its media and communication industry with the support of Shanghai Media & Entertainment Group (SMEG). It has invested into Shanghai Cable Network Co., Ltd. and Eastday.com, the most influential and large-scale network in Shanghai, and Shanghai Oriental TV Station Advertising Co., Ltd. Besides this, it also has invested to gain advertising operating authority during peak time on Shanghai TV, as well as its advertisement operating authority (80% share) for the press media. In October 2002, together with SMEG, OPG set up Shanghai Oriental Pearl Mobile TV Inc., which has developed new media mobile digital TV on air-conditioned buses, ferries and yachts. This new media provides new colourful mobile scenery for the city.

With support of SMEG, OPG will seize the opportunities and make good use of capital market both home and abroad, actively providing its management brand as needed, and is striving to carry out the whole strategy of SMEG as well as culture, radio, film & TV industries in Shanghai.

14.3 Industry network Nottingham

The industry in Nottingham is of a different size and complexity to that in China. Most of the companies fall into the category of SMEs, who have often come from either the closure of larger businesses such as Central TV Studios and Carlton, but have now incubated a number of independent companies in terms of moving image, interactive and media. We already have contacts with many of these companies due to our Foundation degree. The companies are part of a mixed economy which has public and private funding in support of different aspects of their work. The list below includes graphic design, product design, film, games and animation companies, and web design.

14.3.1 Nottingham companies
- Wellington Films
- Bottletop Design
- De Facto Design
- V-Point
- BBC East Midlands – radio and television news and current affairs, broadcasting for the region

- Theatre Writing Partnership
- Broadcast Media Services Nottingham
- EMMedia – media and screen agency for the region
- Detonate
- Broadway Media Centre
- Confetti – film and post-production training centre
- Game City – world games festival
- Seismik
- The Media Company
- Britfilms TV
- Chancenumber Productions
- Martin Knox Branding
- Hot Knife Digital Media - specialising in video production and 3D animation
- Jupiter Design – design communication
- BE Productions
- Linney Group
- Nottingham Playhouse - Theatre
- Monumental Design – Games Design
- Spifire Games Design
- Crytek Games – Games Company
- The Finishing Post
- National Space Science Centre
- Speedo
- Orb and Crash
- Jigsaw Systems – specialist IT supplier
- Toyota
- Together Agency
- Fourmost Films
- Straw Dog - develop applications and games for iPhone, iPad, Android and other Smart Phones, Xbox 360, PlayStation3, Nintendo Wii, 3DS, and PC
- Paul Smith
- Outso - specialise in the creation of high quality virtual environments. We are without equal in terms of track record on Playstation Home.
- One True Saxon – men's fashion wear
- Tribe Graphics
- Little Big Head Mobile Games

- Antenna
- Spool - Dolby approved post-production house

14.3.2 The Hive Start to …

Our 'Hive Start to…' project is the teaching base from which we want to explore these challenges;the purpose of the unit is to develop career opportunities with students. Many universities in the UK have similar sorts of facilities, often called enterprise centres,and they run different length courses which address the forming of a business concept, shaping that business and working as a freelancer. The Hive has mentors who can be attached to particular projects to help the students achieve success in their chosen business field. It has helped create 240 new businesses, and the subsequent generation of more than £8 million in revenue. University graduates and entrepreneurs with viable business ideas have created and run their own companies. Of the businesses launched, an exceptional 85% passed the three year mark and 72% still trade today, employing almost 300 people between them.

The average age of Hive entrepreneurs is 27, and more than 30 have won or reached the finals of major national enterprise competitions since 2006. Businesses launched by Hive entrepreneurs range from fashion and product design, business consultancy services, event management, horticulture and garden design to alternative therapies and social enterprises.

Notable Hive entrepreneurs include Kawsar Miah of wholesale electronics firm Digicom Solutions Ltd, which turned over in excess of £1 million in its first year of trading; the multi-award-winning and market-leading educational software company Prime Principle; and fashion designer and winner of the first ever British Council UK Young Fashion Entrepreneur (UKYFE) Award, Simon Hartwig, who is currently travelling around the USA to promote Nottingham's creative industries.

The Hive offers entrepreneurs a range of programmes to help them get their business off the ground including the 12-week intensive Head Start course, which enables participants to investigate the market, foster a network of business contacts, identify financing opportunities and, where positive potential exists, to start up a company. Hive entrepreneurs also have access to office space, university expertise and on-going mentoring from business experts. Kawsar Miah, who started his business at The Hive while on a

Entrepreneurship for the Creative and Media Arts

Student Placements for Entrepreneurs in Education programme, said:

"The Hive has a brilliant atmosphere for entrepreneurs to gain inspiration. It's the perfect place for someone to understand the true meaning of business and get the support and help needed to make that first leap into starting up their own business."

Chris Hall, business manager at The Hive, said:

"We've defied the ups and downs of the economy and we're delighted to be celebrating an extremely successful ten years. Our support is a recognised role model in Higher Education for graduate and student enterprise and entrepreneurship. We're also a significant driving force in the local economy and, as such, at the forefront of recent government strategies to promote regional equality and economic growth."

Chris Leslie, MP for Nottingham East and shadow financial secretary to the Treasury, recently visited The Hive to discover how it contributes to business and the creative industries in Nottingham. He added:

"It is vitally important that we encourage and support new enterprise in Nottingham if we are to continue developing a sustainable and competitive local economy. The creative, digital and information technology (CDIT) sector offers an amazing opportunity for the city to further diversify its economy and gain its share of a global CDIT market worth an estimated $3 trillion. The Hive has played a crucial role in aiding the development of start-up businesses in this sector by enabling highly skilled university graduates to make the often difficult transition into enterprise. Through supporting the entrepreneurs of today, The Hive is helping to create the businesses of tomorrow, driving forward the innovation that will secure a prosperous future for Nottingham's economy."

An example of this success is the company Orb & Crash. Jonathan Hawley and Jay Ludditt built their company after they joined The Hive's HeadStart programme, just as their studies in design were coming to an end. "The process of preparing the business plan was more useful than the actual plan itself – it almost instantly became out of date," said Jay. "However, setting targets and discussing issues like finance and marketing enabled us to take a very realistic view of our business prospects. Thankfully we were used to living on a shoestring from our student days and, with the help of The Hive, we embarked on a progressive learning curve." Orb & Crash was launched from a spare room at home with just one computer between the two of them. Both continued with part-time jobs in the early days and retained their contact with The Hive through the SmarTrak programme of long-term mentoring. "It really was starting from scratch – every little job meant a bit more money to invest in the business," explained Jon. "Networking through The Hive was useful for generating work opportunities, giving us valuable exposure and learning from the other entrepreneurs. The on-going mentoring we've received has also given us extra impetus as well as time to pause and reflect."

Specialising in branding, graphic design, packaging and digital media, Jay and Jon secured their first major design contract with a catering equipment supplier and their client list has grown dramatically since. Orb & Crash have a distinctive approach of harnessing creativity with a long-term strategic vision; ensuring brands resonate with target audiences and drive businesses forward. Within a year of setting up they had moved into a studio in Mansfield and now have upmarket offices in the heart of Nottingham – a symbol of how far their agency has advanced. "Having been in business for almost five years, we are fully independent but know we can rely on The Hive for advice when we need it," Jay commented. Ultimate plans are for Orb & Crash to make its mark in London, but the duo is determined to retain the approachability, honesty and openness with which they have made their name. "Our success is based on longstanding client relationships. Companies choose us because we make them feel valued and take the time to understand their business. There's no pretending we don't aspire to be a bigger name, but we want to distinguish ourselves from agencies where clients might feel their projects get lost," says Jon. Keen to 'give something back'; Jay and Jon have delivered talks at The Hive to share their own entrepreneurial experiences. They also help foster the talents of young creative individuals by mentoring, teaching and running workshops at local colleges and universities.

Another example of a small business success is Detonate. Detonate is a small company established in 1999 by NTU graduate James Busby. The company is based in offices above the Golden Fleece on Mansfield Road and it promotes and organises music nights, festivals and individual gigs in the area. The company uses a range of media to promote its product and is always looking at expanding its loyal fan base. It organises the Detonate

Indoor Festival (Rock City, Stealth, Rescue Rooms and EQ), regular Detonate and Basslaced events at Stealth and Dogma Presents every Thursday. The company hires venues, books talent and markets events via the web, SMS, social networks and a range of other promotional material. The company is now at an exciting stage in its development as it plans for the next three years of activity, building on strong partnerships and developing new strands of work.

This virtuous circle illustrated by these two companies is what we are striving to develop between our groups of students in Shanghai and Nottingham.

14.4 Our sharing initiatives – The Next Stage

So far we have mapped the current practices and outlined exposure that students get to what we might call entrepreneurial experiences; they have also shared work in a collaborative digital media and photography project. NTU staff have presented ways of thinking about being an entrepreneur in the arts and creative media, and as part of our visit we demonstrated some of the thinking that lies behind The Hive Start To… programme.

This was well received and sparked debate about the types of work the SIVA students wished to undertake. As in the UK, successes are often borne out by the drive and motivation of the individual. Our next task is to translate some of the instinctive approaches in Art and Design that make people effective entrepreneurs. These attributes include conceptual thinking, risk taking, planning, failing and reflection. We have spoken with students and graduates at length about their work and aspirations.

It is clear from the background of these activities that students at both institutions have an understanding of the relevance of their work in both business and societal contexts, and that they are given exposure of their creative work in commercial contexts. It was important from this sharing that we try to discover how an incubation environment could be set up to encourage creative business generation, where the students and graduates develop their businesses.

Reflecting on our shared work so far, we do have appropriate alignments of activities, particularly with SIVAs Integrated Design Studio and the Business Planning workshop and NTU's Entrepreneur module development and The

Hive courses. It is from this base that we intend, in year 2 of the PMI project, to develop a shared programme of Entrepreneurial materials and spaces.

Our targets now involve creating the curriculum and incubator space both for face-to-face and online business building. We want to take the concepts explored in these areas and develop our shared vision for the entrepreneur in the global market, embracing the arts and entrepreneurship.

We hope to encourage some exchange of Chinese design for film and TV so that it is exhibited alongside our student work at Pinewood and, in return, our students will be exhibited to the Shanghai Media Group. In Nottingham, we have a PhD research student who is exploring cultural animation production and will share research ideas. These liaisons go some way to building both our relationships and future companies.

As has been identified in the preceding sections, media content is a likely space for development and so we hope to start a project called *Content without Walls* for the sharing of materials between the two institutions. We began to share some of this work in 2009, but have been also negotiating shared space that can be accessed by both sets of students and staff. This blog and forum space is integral to the formation of the incubator units. With this work we would aim to share and develop iPhone and android apps in order to showcase the art work from both countries. This year we have also launched an Award for Shanghai-Nottingham Entrepreneurship to encourage collaborative endeavour, and we are linking up with a Shanghai artist who has also set up a gallery in the hope of exchanging artefacts and exhibitions between his works and those of Tether and Moot.

Ultimately, the next stage in this process will take time and effort in order to share ideas and project work but, more importantly, different ways of encouraging ideas and a safe place to share.It is this iterative process that artists bring to the development of work that can, eventually, succeed.

> *"I have not failed. I've just found 10,000 ways that won't work."*
> (Thomas Edison, inventor and scientist)

15 Enhancing Employability Through Life-Wide Learning – The Plymouth University Model

David Croot, Associate Professor and University Teaching Fellow, Plymouth University, UK

Plymouth University is in the vanguard of sector-wide changes to the undergraduate experience, particularly focused on graduate employability. We employ an over-arching principle of understanding graduate employability to be more than a set of skills and competencies developed within curricula or taught programmes and we have adopted the following definition of graduate employability:

> *"....having a set of skills, knowledge, understanding and personal attributes that make a person more likely to choose and secure occupations in which they can be satisfied and successful"* (Dacre, Pool and Sewell, 2007)

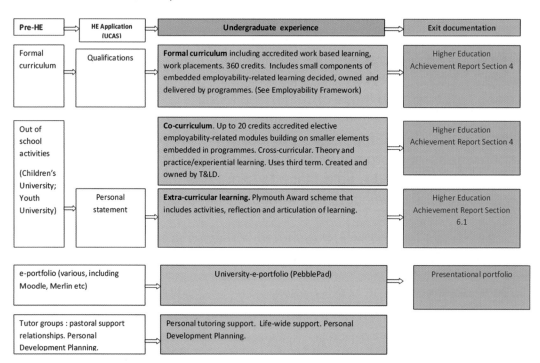

Figure 15.1 Model of the pre-HE and undergraduate/PGT experience for the University of Plymouth

Our model of the student experience journey, illustrated in Figure 15.1 comprises a number of stages and elements:

15.1 Stage progression

Pre-H.E - We acknowledge that many students enter UK higher education without clear career goals, so part of our mission is to help students identify their personal strengths and set appropriate career aspirations which are not necessarily related to their chosen degree programme. Many students select an undergraduate discipline for study simply because they have excelled in that discipline in pre-H.E educational settings, or they find the subject interesting and stimulating.

At University - The employability of our graduates depends on many factors. Dacre Pool and Sewell (2007) suggest that employability is based on reflection, evaluation and learning from a combination of discipline and career development learning, work and life experience, and the development of generic skills and emotional intelligence.

Whilst many graduate qualities are developed within the context of the academic discipline as integral to the learning associated with that discipline, there are many that are not consciously developed or are part of the learning outcomes of the programme.

We differentiate between those qualities that are particularly developed in the context of the discipline and those more generic qualities that are probably best assimilated/acquired through specific interventions that we might collectively describe as "career development learning".

Career development learning helps students to make informed decisions about their future career and to successfully secure their chosen role. It involves an understanding of self, including strengths and preferences, an understanding of available opportunities, skills in decision making, and the practical skills to successfully compete in the recruitment process.

There are many theories and models underpinning career development learning but one of the most enduring is the DOTS Model (Law & Watts, 1977). It provides a straightforward view of the core elements of successful career development learning and how these interconnect. The DOTS Model is based on four components (Figure 15.2).

Figure 15.2 DOTS

(Source, Law and Watts, 1977)

As with any academic discipline, careers education can be benchmarked against learning outcomes. The following table (15.1) summarises the Careers Education benchmarking statement for all graduates with reference to the DOTS model above. It is endorsed by the Higher Education Academy, the Association of Graduate Recruiters, and the Centre for Recording Achievement, the Standing Committee of Principals, the Careers Research and Advisory Centre, Association of Graduate Careers Advisory Services and the Higher Education Careers Service Unit.

Table 15.1 Careers education benchmark statement criteria

Threshold students will be able to:	Exemplary students in addition will be able to:
Assess their strengths and weaknesses and Identify broad areas for personal growth and development (self-awareness)	Identify specific skills, qualifications and experience requiring further development
Demonstrate an understanding of the general requirements of graduate recruiters and the value they place on work experience and other extra- curricular activities (opportunity awareness)	Describe in detail the specific entry requirements for the options relevant to their career plans
Identify the key elements of effective career decision making (decision making)	Inform their planning using an understanding of their own decision-making style(s)
Identify the specific challenges and obstacles to their success in securing and developing within an opportunity (transition learning)	Deploy appropriate behaviours to adapt successfully to their new environment

Providing students with opportunities to access and develop their skills and attributes through creating opportunities for self-reflection and evaluation of these experiences within and beyond the curriculum, results in our students achieving high levels of self-efficacy, self-confidence and self-esteem; which are crucial building blocks for employability.

To get the jobs they desire, graduates need to be able to provide evidence of their graduate skills and attributes in the recruitment and selection process: on application forms and CVs, at assessment centres and in interview situations. In these situations, students are typically asked to 'provide an example of a time when ...', requiring them to draw on a range of examples from their programme, work experience, extra-curricular activities, etc. that provide the essential, authentic evidence that they can "walk the walk" as well as "talk the talk".

Furthermore, to be successful in the recruitment and selection process students not only need experience to draw upon, but to be able to reflect on what they have learned from these experiences and to articulate this learning to employers. Making clear to students that reflection activities are degree-relevant and workplace-relevant is, in our view, very important.

Generic skills are those typically referred to by employers as 'soft' or 'transferable' skills. There are many lists and definitions of graduate level skills and attributes required by employers. The following is a typical summary of these skills and attributes in four areas:

1. Self-reliance skills e.g. self-awareness, willingness to learn, enthusiasm.

2. People skills e.g. team working, interpersonal skills, leadership, language skills.

3. General employment skills e.g. problem solving, flexibility, business acumen, computer literacy.

4. Specialist skills e.g. specific occupational or technical skills.

At Plymouth we have developed a strategy for implementing employability which differentiates roles and responsibilities of the delivery programme teams and central core services based on the model in Figure 15.1. Many employability skills, competencies, attributes and dispositions are developed and practiced within the context of the student's academic programme and we have set a minimum entitlement of employability education which students can reasonably expect to receive within their programme.

Within-programme employability development - Whilst we have set out what students can reasonably expect to receive within their programme of study, we have not set out which part of the University should facilitate this learning, how that learning should be delivered, or whether it should be assessed as part of the programme curriculum. We have suggested that all these aspects (facilitating learning, delivery styles, assessment etc.) are best developed as a collaborative process which engages programme staff, our Careers and Employability Service, employers, alumni and students. We also offer several delivery models for these stakeholder groups to discuss and develop in the context of their own practice.

A significant amount of employability learning already occurs within programmes, and all our students are expected to develop the following attributes within the programme of study:

1. Written communication skills to their full potential.

2. Numeracy skills as appropriate.

3. Presentation skills for different audiences using different media.

4. Group work skills: basic theory and practice.

5. Gather, critically evaluate, analyse and synthesise information as appropriate.

6. Critical thinking skills.

7. Problem solving skills.

8. Decision making skills.

9. Practical skills as appropriate to the discipline.

10. An understanding of the graduate labour market, including clear explanation of the previous 3 years of graduate destinations data, types of destination organisations, initial career paths and starting salaries.

11. The value of timely career planning and the steps required to do this effectively.

12. How to research an organisation to which students might apply for a graduate position.

13. The importance of taking extra-curricular opportunities that Plymouth University offers (and graduate recruiters require of graduates).

14. Opportunities to engage in work-related learning appropriate to the discipline through a range of strategies.

Whilst the majority of these qualities are common to undergraduate programmes across the sector in the UK, we place special emphasis on some of the above. For example:

- Understanding the labour market and different career options available (#9 above). Graduates have a wide range of careers options and understanding these is key to making informed career choices. Many graduate employers do not specify particular disciplines when recruiting; and while some programmes are vocational, with a high proportion of their students having a specific career track in mind (e.g. teaching, health care, social work), others provide a broad based platform for a diverse range of careers (e.g. environmental sciences, geography, history, English). UK graduate destinations data shows very clearly that even those who commence their undergraduate study in a vocational area often do not directly enter a career in that discipline area, so understanding the diverse range of careers which previous graduates have entered is important knowledge.

- The value of timely career planning. (#10 above). In an increasingly competitive graduate career market, students need to be made aware of the value attached to career planning. The majority of students are not open to these ideas until they have settled into the university and their discipline. Many also leave career planning much too late in their undergraduate experience. Evidence shows that the best time to begin stimulating thinking about careers is towards the end of stage 1 and into stage 2. Many staff can play a role in this process but the principle one in our model will be the personal tutor. We have established this as part of the role of the personal tutor within our personal tutoring policy.

- Researching employment sectors (#11 above). Opportunity awareness of the DOTS model above. Feedback from graduate employers repeatedly stresses that graduates are often ill prepared for rigorous application and selection processes. Researching potential sectors and employers is a critical primary step in this process because it enables students to match their skills and aptitudes to the requirements of the posts and the role/job descriptions. (Of course this is based on an assumption that students know themselves sufficiently well to be able to match themselves to available opportunities.) This self-awareness is embedded within the personal tutoring policy as a student entitlement.

- The importance of taking extra-curricular opportunities (#12 above). It is impossible to underestimate the value of life-wide experience in addition to a good degree when graduates are seeking employment, whatever the career aspiration. This philosophy and strategy is explored in more detail below.

- Opportunities to engage in work-related learning (#13 above). Many academic programmes, whether vocational or non-vocational, already provide opportunities for students to engage in work-related learning. These opportunities may range from short observational experiences through to year-long placements. They may be assessed, or not, as appropriate. They may be paid or voluntary. From the perspective of graduate employability, the more work-related learning students can accumulate the better placed they are to present themselves for graduate careers with an authentic set of experiences.

We strive to ensure that the development of all the above occurs through a combination of one or more of the following strategies within the main programme of study.

1. Embedded sessions in modules threaded through existing provision, linked to the most appropriate content at the most appropriate stage. This approach offers most flexibility with learning assessed within existing modules.

2. A stand-alone careers module, usually in Stage 2 or 3.

3. Career Management Days, planned and possibly delivered in conjunction with the Careers & Employability Service. These days can cover the main aspects of career management, particularly if staged at intervals throughout a programme.

4. Mixed models, which deliver employability through a mixture of the above.

15.2 Extra-curricular employability learning development: putting meaning into life-wide learning

The concept of Life-wide Learning has been thoroughly treated by a number of authorities over the years. The most recent and authoritative UK treatment is Jackson's (2011) "Learning for a complex world". Life-wide learning is predicated on the notion that our lives are complete experiences and that we naturally transfer learning from one "silo" to another unless we are forced into a silo mentality by cultural imperatives. Our mission at Plymouth is to encourage students to realise that their lives are not compartmentalised and that their employability is strongly based on a) recognising a boundary-less approach to learning, b) the ability to draw on these life-wide experiences to exemplify their employability, c) to be able to reflect on these experiences and draw learning from all of them, and d) to be able to articulate that learning in a career setting.

Plymouth University is therefore committed to providing an exceptional menu of opportunities from which all students are invited to select ones to suit them. This scale and value of this offer sets Plymouth apart from the majority of HEIs and every student is strongly encouraged to avail themselves of as many of these as possible.

In broad terms, we offer two strands of opportunities outside the formal curriculum: a) the Plymouth Award scheme (see http://www.plymouth.ac.uk/plymouthaward) and b) a menu of co-curricular mini-modules which carry academic credit but sit outside the student's own curriculum. These modules include, for example, group-work, teamwork, employer/employee relations, organisational structures, representing others, cultural awareness, languages, multi-cultural societies and groups, sustainability, health and safety at work, risk analysis, environmental assessments, time management, language skills, application of numeracy, digital literacy, effective communication skills, negotiating skills, business awareness and so on. These extra-curricular opportunities are drawn together into a consistent framework which students are able to navigate, identifying and taking opportunities that particularly suit them and their embryonic career aspirations.

15.3 Exit documentation

The UK Higher Education system undertook a review of the exit documentation which accompanies graduation. This review, chaired by Sir Bob Burgess, recommended the adoption of a new style of exit document called the Higher Education Achievement Report (HEAR) to replace the out-dated simple degree classification system used hitherto (Beyond the honours degree classification, Burgess Group Final Report, Universities UK, 2007). The HEAR will replace the current transcript and include information included in the European Diploma supplement (EDS). The majority of UK Universities are in the process of developing HEARs and most will produce these documents by 2013. One of the most significant improvements compared with previous exit documentation will be the ability to include verified achievements outside the main formal programme of study. Thus Plymouth will be able to include not only details of achievements within the programme of study, but also the extra-curricular award and any co-curricular employability-enhancing modules taken on an optional basis by students. The HEAR does not displace presentational portfolios, CV's or application forms for graduate positions, but it does provide a vehicle for graduates to showcase their life-wide achievements. It also gives the University a clear rationale for stressing the importance of life-wide learning to incoming and existing students to their future employability.

16 Concluding Remarks

Employability emerged from the literature as an issue of growing importance in the modern academic setting; increased numbers and greater competition inherently means that candidates must stand out. That these skills vary by both discipline and cultural setting seems logical, and again emerges from the coherent literature around the topic. Primary data reported in the preceding results chapters examined these issues in both a UK and Chinese context and represents a rigorous and broad study of employability characteristics in the two countries. This chapter concludes this book by examining some of the emergent themes and links these to the broader literature.

The first section of this book sought to situate employability within the current literature and to clarify the variances which are present when integrating these skills into university level courses. The theory and practice of employability was also outlined. Higher education in both the UK and China has expanded at extraordinarily fast rates, clearly leading to a more competitive job market in both countries. Employability thus becomes a central issue. The term employability was itself outlined in the first section and was taken to include the skills, achievements and personal attributes of successful graduates:

> "...a set of achievements – skills, understandings and personal attributes – that make graduates more likely to gain employment and be successful in their chosen occupations, which benefits themselves, the workforce, the community and the economy".
> (Enhancing Student Employability Coordination Team (ESECT), 2003, p.4.)

These skills and attributes were subsequently discussed in detail, with specific references to the current literature around employability. In Chapter 3, we examined ways in which these skills could be integrated and implemented into university teaching material. We proposed a model of integrative support structures which must be in place to aid this integration, as well as suggesting potential barriers. The section concluded by examining the variance of employability skills across disciplines, delivery and, more broadly, cultures. Learning, as well as employment itself, clearly changes across cultures; thus employability skills delivery should also.

Section B was a direct examination of these issues through the rigorous collection, analysis and interpretation of primary data. The large-scale research conducted consisted of 60 interviews with key individuals across three disciplines (marketing, finance and HR), and two countries. These interview data revealed interesting similarities and differences and it is these that were expanded upon in subsequent sections to comprise the rest of this chapter. These data also made it possible to suggest discipline and culturally specific strategies for integration.

Section C was potentially the most important section of the book. We presented case studies to illustrate all of the issues raised in the first two sections. These represent a snapshot of the current thinking in H.E around cutting edge employability integration. The introduction of an MSc at Plymouth University, which has employability at its heart, illuminated the integration model proposed in Chapter 3, whilst contributions from London College of Fashion and the University of Northampton showed to what level innovative and creative strategies have developed. Imperial College offered a report of the novel use of summer schools in order to target an often neglected group in terms of employability; PhD students. Nottingham Trent University and the Shanghai Institute of Visual Arts presented a joint case study of collaborative work towards employability which also best encapsulates the themes in this book. Lastly, a final study from Plymouth University explored the strategic and specific application of a model of employability at the university.

Before examining some differences and similarities, it is worth briefly considering the total, broad scale findings across all three sub-disciplines and two cultures. Almost all of the respondents mentioned communicative skills in some form or another as being fundamentally important to the successful employability of students. Across all measures employers reported wanting people who could communicate well both verbally and in written work. This is clearly an important finding and the rigorousness of the research implies that one would expect to find the same attitudes in the broader work market. The coherent integration of developing communication skills into all levels of delivery and assessment is therefore one of the key suggestions made by this book. University level educators, from lecturing staff to strategic managers, should identify creative and innovative ways to deepen students' skills in this field. It is important to note however that communication skills are not just written; verbal forms such as networking, persuading and selling were also seen as key.

Additionally, though less strongly, organisational skills alongside a person's persona and commercial knowledge all emerged as key themes which should be highlighted by candidates if they are to be competitive in the job market. Whilst less operationalisable than communicative skills, these are elements which should become more central in courses aiming to deliver high calibre business graduates. Strategies which introduce these skills at an early stage and develop them more specifically include providing students with up to date business news, extra-curricular activities and personal action planning.

Between disciplines there was certainly some general level of cohesiveness, aside from the ubiquitous communication skills, employers from all three fields reported the importance of commercial acumen and organisation in particular. It was unsurprising that candidates were required to have a good working knowledge of the particular discipline in question; a finding which vindicates both advanced study modules and work-experience/ related learning. University

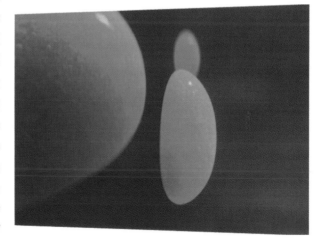

courses often have elements linked to work experience in some form and the finding in this instance demonstrates the importance of continuing with this trend. Again unsurprisingly, a well organised student was a highly employable one; for course designers and delivery staff strategies which place the emphasis on individual learning should rightly be adopted. The skills which emerged conformed, largely, to those present in the literature. Readers seeking further explanations and integration techniques would be advised to explore the chapters (divided into skills sections) in Hind and Moss (2011).

However, there were also differences between disciplines which highlight the need for highly tailored and specific strategies which vary according to subject area. In the current research, what emerged was that the *emphases* varied greatly between disciplines; whilst the overall skills were largely consistent, the importance placed on each element was different for each area. Marketing and HR, as more people orientated areas, highlighted the need for personable and highly communicative individuals who could problem solve. Conversely, financial employers emphasised the need for commercial and business acumen and the need for highly developed sensitivity for the world of business.

Necessarily such differences reflect the disciplines themselves as much as the employers who were interviewed. The implications for integrating these skills into education strategies are clear; there would be considerable variance between modules, programmes and individual elements. Whilst it may be beneficial for finance undergraduates to have increased levels of data protection training, students from HR may well be better served by having group scenario sessions.

Between China and the UK there were also differences in emphases placed on certain characteristics for potential employers. In marketing and finance, for example, the emphasis by employers in the UK was on recruiting candidates who conformed to a pre-existing role profile and had the ability to work as part of a team. However, the same discipline interviews in China yielded responses more focused on individual excellence and the raw talent of a candidate. Honesty, integrity and issues of privacy emerged from the Chinese interviews with more strength than those in the UK. Though it should be noted that in interviews with HR employers, there was little difference between the two cultures, with both indicating a need for organised and personable employees.

It is not the purpose of this section to re-list the results from the preceding chapters; the elements of difference between disciplines and cultures emerge from these data with striking clarity. The implications for both the delivery of employability at university level and the employability literature more broadly are significant.

It is hard to overstate the level of importance which should be assigned to reliable, valid and robust integration of employability skills for graduates; the rise in unemployment in this demograp-hic further enhances the need for incre-ased individual competitiveness in the market. Universities remain, as the De-partment for Business, Innovation and Skills (2012) highlight, a key part of the supply chain for business; making graduate employability ever more cent-

ral. The findings from this study contribute to the growing literature on employability skills integration (Knight and Yorke, 2004; Yorke, 2004) and, more specifically, suports those who have argued for differentiating specificity and skills by culture and discipline (Young, 2010). What the significant data in this instance show is that the impact of individual teaching staff on employability development is great, and that innovativeness at this level is therefore central (see Heffernan et al., 2009; Sweeney et al., 2009).

This brings us back to the model of integration introduced in Chapter three; data reported here vindicate such a model for the comprehensive delivery of these skills. Lecturing staff must be actively creative within both the delivery and assessment of material (Sweeney et al., 2009). However, this creativity and innovation can only be effective if supported by broader mechanisms from the institutions (at module and programme levels) and wider strategic/social support.

The main message from the results reported here is that there are important lessons to be learned from cross-cultural analyses of employability skills; certainly in this case there were significant differences observed between the Chinese and UK students. These findings have implications for the employability literature more broadly, especially around marketing, finance and HR. Those individuals involved in the delivery of employability skills should consider cultural differences at all stages. Certainly in the theme of Jackson's (2011) conceptions of life-wide learning: that many spheres of life contribute to employability. More holistic approaches are certainly a key finding which we would support.

Whilst more research is certainly warranted, there are some claims from these data which can be made. It could be hypothesised that most disciplines and cultures will exhibit important differences in terms of employability characteristics, or at the very least in employability skills focus and emphasis. This is a finding in keeping with the literature, and the scale of the research reported in this book lends some weight behind these notions (see Young, 2010; Baker and Henson, 2010).

The key similarities which were noted between sub-disciplines are applicable to the wider education sector and are of use for alternative fields. These transferrable skills (see Petrova and Ujma, 2006) are often under-valued in self-assessments by students and the current research highlights this issue.

It would be, again, hard to overstate the importance of the less specific (but still certainly concrete) skills identified by almost all employers as important for increased competitiveness in the market. It is these personality traits, including motivation and enthusiasm amongst others, which have been demonstrated to be valued less than subject specifics by students (Petrova and Ujma, 2006). This is clearly an issue which should now be at the forefront as a key way to better inform and improve students from a range of cultural backgrounds and subject disciplines.

One of the main points readers should take from this book is the focus on individual members of teaching staff and their ability to be able to integrate employability skills through innovative, creative and different formats, which is the primary feature of highly employable individuals. The supportive model proposed in the earlier chapters of this book is vindicated by the subsequent primary data collection and the illustrative case studies. Overwhelmingly, the indications are (from all sections of this book) that students are entering an ever more competitive market which is also increasingly crowded; these students need to be sure that they are being given the correct skills in order to be successful.

Overall, we hope that this book has given some idea of the current debates around employability and its importance in both the UK and Chinese higher education systems. We have aimed to explore the theory and practice of employability within these systems through the literature in the field, primary research and some illuminating case study reports. By exploring these areas it is hoped that the reader is better informed as to the theoretical debates and their application in the current education systems. We have sought to raise awareness and flag key issues around employability as much as we have answered important questions through research. Whilst the strategies provided in the results sections should certainly be used as guidance for on-going employability development, it is our hope that readers are encouraged to further develop these ideas in their own fields. The themes which have emerged as central to all of the chapters and cases presented here are certainly those which will become ever more important as the competition in the job market increases; something which seems likely in both China and the UK.

References

6Xueinfo. (2006).'University Education in China.'Available at: http://www.6xue.info. Accessed: 10.10.08.

Ackers, L. (2004).'Managing relationships in peripatetic careers: Scientific mobility in the European Union.'*Women's Studies International Forum,27,* 3, pp.189-201.

Alpay E, Walsh E. (2008).'A skills perception inventory for evaluating postgraduate transferable skills development.'*Assessment and Evaluation in Higher Education, 33,* pp.581-598.

Andrews, J. and Higson, H. (2008). "Graduate employability, 'soft skills' versus 'hard' business knowledge: a European study." *Higher Education in Europe,33,4,* pp. 411-422.

Astin, A. W. (1997). "How 'good' is your institution's retention rate?" *Research in Higher Education, 38,*6, pp. 647-658.

Atkins, M.J. (1999) 'Oven-ready and self-basting: taking stock of employability skills', *Teaching in Higher Education, 4,*2, pp. 267-280.

Australian Chamber of Commerce and Industry & Business Council of Australia.(2002).'Employability Skills for the Future.' Canberra: Department of Education, Science & Training. Available at: http://www.usq.edu.au/beyondeducation/employability/skills. Accessed 10.11.11.

Australian Government (2005).'Unlocking China's service sector.'Canberra: Dept. of Foreign Affairs and Trade. Available at:http://www.dfat.gov.au/publications/eau_unlocking_china/unlocking_china_services.pdf. Accessed 11.11.11.

Baker, G. and Henson, D. (2010).'Promoting employability skills development in a research-intensive University', *Education and Training.52,* 1, pp. 62-75

BBC News [online], (2010). 'David Cameron launches Tories' 'big society' plan'. Available at: http://www.bbc.co.uk/news/uk-10680062 Accessed: 2.12.11.

Berg, B. (1989), *Qualitative research methods for the social sciences. 5th edn,* Pearson: London.

Biggs, J. (1991).'Asian learners through western eyes: An astigmatic paradox', *Australian and New Zealand Journal of Vocational Education Research, 2, 2,* pp. 40-63.

Biggs, J.B. (1996). 'Western misconceptions of the Confucian-heritage learning culture', in Watkins, D.A., Biggs, J.B. (Eds),*The Chinese Learner: Cultural, Psychological and Contextual Influences,* Hong Kong: CERC and ACER.

Bloxham, S. (2005).*Embedding skills and employability in higher education: an institutional curriculum framework approach.* The Higher Education Academy, Working Paper.

Boles, W., Pillay, H. and Raj, L. (1999).'Marching cognitive styles to computer-based instruction: An approach for enhanced learning in electrical engineering.'*European Journal of Engineering Education, 24,* 4, pp. 371-383.

Brent, J. and Kraska, P. (2010), 'Moving beyond our methodological default: a case for mixed methods.' *Journal of Criminal Justice Education, 21,* 4, pp. 412-430.

British Council [online] (n.d.) 'The Prime Minister's Initiative for International Education.'London: British Council. Available at: http://www.britishcouncil.org/eumd-pmi2.htm. Accessed: 15.11.10.

Brown, P., Hesketh, A., and Williams, S. (2003).'Employability in a Knowledge-driven Economy', *Journal of Education and Work, 16, 2,* pp. 107-126.

Burnapp, D. and Zhao, W. (2009). 'Voices from the chat rooms: research into the experiences of Chinese students participating in transnational education programmes as reported on internet social networks.' *Enhancing the Learner Experience in Higher Education,1,*1,pp. 30-43.

CBI, (2009).*Future Fit: Preparing graduates for the world of work,* London: Confederation of British Industry.

CBI, (2010).*Education and Skills Survey 2010.*London: Confederation of British Industry.

Chan, S. (1999).'The Chinese learning – A question of style',*Education and Training, 41,*6/7, pp. 294-304.

Charkins, R.J., O'Toole, D.M. and Wetzel, J.N. (1985).'Linking teaching and student learning styles with student achievement and attitudes',*Journal of Economic Education,16,* pp. 111-120.

Chen, J. (1979).*The history of China's modern education.*Beijing: People's education press.

China's Central Government. (2010). Outline of National Mid and Long TermEducation Development and Reform Plan 2010-2020 [Online]. Available at: http://www.gov.cn/jrzg/2010-07/29/content_1667143.htm Accessed: 7.3.12.

CIHE (2005).*Student Employability Profiles; A Guide for Employers.* London: CIHE.

CIHE (2006).*Student Employability Profiles; A Guide for Higher Education Practitioners.* London: CIHE.

CIPD Factsheet.[online] (2010). 'Coaching and Mentoring', CIPD. Available at:http://www.cipd.co.uk/subjects/lrnanddev/coachmntor/coaching. htm?IsSrchRes=1. Accessed: 2.12.11.

Cortazzi, M. and Jin, L. (1996). 'Cultures of Learning: Language Classrooms in China', In Coleman H. (Ed.), *Society and the Language Classroom.* Melbourne: Cambridge University Press.

Covey, S. (2004). *The 7 Habits of Highly Effective People.* London: Simon and Schuster.

Creswell, J. (2007). *Qualitative inquiry and research design; choosing among five approaches.* London: Sage.

Cushman, D. P. and King, S. (1985). 'National and organizational cultures in conflict resolution: Japan, the United Sates, and Yugoslavia', in Gudycunst, W., Stewart, L. and Ting-Toomey, S. (eds.). *Communication, Culture, and Organizational Processes,* Beverly Hills: Sage.

Dacre Pool, L. and Sewell, P. (2007). *The key to employability: developing a practical model of graduate employability.* Centre for Employability: University of Central Lancashire.

DCMS, (2007). *Staying ahead: the economic performance of the UK's creative industries.* London: Department for Culture, Media and Sport.

De Grip, A., Van Loo, J., and Sanders, J. (2004). 'The Industry Employability Index: Taking account of supply and demand characteristics', *International Labour Review, 143*,3, pp. 212-233.

Department for Business, Innovation and Skills, (2012). *A Review of Business-University Collaboration.* London: Department for Business, Innovation and Skills.

DfES (2003). *The future of Higher Education. White Paper on Higher Education',* London: Department for Education and Skills.

Department of Education, Science and Training, (2005). *A National Quality Strategy for Australian Transnational Education and Training*: A Discussion Paper. Canberra: Commonwealth of Australia.

Diaz, D. P., and Cartnal, R. B. (1999). 'Students' learning styles in two classes: Online distance learning and equivalent on-campus', *College Teaching, 47*,4, pp. 130-135.

Ding, D., Goodall, K. and Warner, M. (2000). 'The end of the 'iron rice-bowl': whither Chinese human resource management?' *The International Journal of Human Resource Management,11*, 2, pp. 217-236.

Editorial Board of China Education Yearbook. 1949-1981, 1982-1984, 1990, 2000, 2001, 2002, 2003, 2004, 2005, 2006. *China Education Yearbook.* Beijing: People's Education Press. (in Chinese).

Erasmus TOTAL. (2011). Available at: http://ec.europa.eu/education/erasmus/doc920_en.htmAccessed: 2.12.11.

Entwistle, N. andTait, H. (1994).*The revised approach to studying inventory.* Centre for Research into Learning and Instruction: University of Edinburgh.

Fallows, S., and Steven, C. (2000).'Building employability skills into higher education curriculum: A university-wide initiative', *Education & Training, 42*, 2, pp. 75-82.

Fang, Z., and Xie, C. (2006).'Exploring the employability and its training model', *Sun Yatsen University Forum, 26*,8, pp. 195-199.

Felder, R.M. (1993). 'Reaching the second tier: Learning and teaching styles in college science education',*Journal of College Science Teaching, 23*, 5, pp. 286-290.

Felder, R.M. and Silverman, L. K., (1988). 'Learning and teaching styles in engineering education',*Engineering Education ,78*,7, pp. 674-781.

Felder, R.M., and Soloman, B.A., [online] (2004). 'Index of learning styles', Available at:http://www.ncsu.edu/felderpublic/ILSpage.html.Accessed: 04.11.11.

Fenton, S. (2010).*Ethnicity: Key Concepts.* Cambridge: Polity.

Fletcher, R., and Bohn, J. (1998).'The impact of psychic distance on the internationalisation of the Australian firm',*Journal of Global Marketing, 12*,2, pp. 47-68.

Gedye, S. and Chalkley, B (2006).*Employability within Geography, Earth and Environmental Science;GEES Learning and Teaching Guide.* HEA GEES Subject Centre: University of Plymouth.

Global People,[online] (2010). 'Global People - supporting intercultural partnerships.', Warwick University. Available at: http://www2.warwick.ac.uk/fac/cross_fac/globalpeople/. Accessed: 15.11.10.

Godula, G., Li, D., and Yu, R. [online] (2009).'Chinese Social Networks 'Virtually' Out-Earn Facebook And MySpace: A Market Analysis.'Techcrunch. Available at: http://www.techcrunch.com/2009/04/05/chinese-social-networks-virtually-out-earn-facebook-and-myspace-a-market-analysis/. Accessed: 17.06.09.

Green, G. [online] (1999).'The British University Before And During The Nineteenth Century', Working Paper. Available at: http://www.ggreentuition.co.uk/pdf/short%20history%20british%20university.pdf. Accessed: 5.12.11.

Guo, P. (2009). 'Study of the employment ability of university graduates and counter-measures.' *Journal of Yangzhaou University (Higher Education Edition).13,* 1,pp. 63-65.

Haldane, A. (2010). 'The contribution of the financial sector; miracle or mirage?'*The Future of Finance Conference 2010.* London. 14th July 2010.

Harvey, L. (1997).*Graduate:Work.* Birmingham: Centre for Research into Quality, University of Central England.

Harvey, L. (1999).*Employability Audit Toolkit.* Birmingham: Centre for Research into Quality.

Harvey, L. (2005).'Embedding and Integrating Employability', *New Directions For Institutional Research, 128,* pp. 13-28.

Hawkins, P. (1999).*The Art of Building Windmills.* Liverpool: Graduate into Employablilty Unit, University of Liverpool.

Heffernan, T. W., Morrison, M., and Sweeney, A. (2006),'Learning Styles and Transnational Education: The Chinese-Australian Question', A refereed paper at the *Australian and New Zealand Marketing Academy Conference.* 4-6 December, Brisbane, Queensland, Australia.

Heffernan, T., Morrison, M, Sweeney, A. and Jarratt, D. (2009). 'Personal attributes of effective lecturers: The importanceof dynamism, communication, rapport and applied knowledge.' *International Journal of Management Education.8,* 3, pp.13-27.

Heffernan, T, Morrison, M, Basu, P and Sweeney, A. (2010). 'Cultural differences, learning styles and transnational education', *Journal of Higher Education Policy and Management, 32,* 1, pp. 27-39.

Higher Education Statistics Agency.(2011). *Destinations of Leavers from Higher Education.*DLHE. Available at:http://www.hesa.ac.uk/index.php?option=com_content&task=view&id=1899&Itemid=239. Accessed 25.10.11.

Hillage, J., and Pollard, E. (1998).*Employability: Developing a Framework For Policy Analysis,* London: Department for Education and Employment.

Hind, D. and Moss, S. (2011). *Employability Skills (2nded.).* Sunderland: Business Education Publishers.

Hofstede, G. (1994). Cultural constraints in management theories. *International Review of Strategic Management, 5,* pp. 27-49.

Hofstede, G. (1980).*Cultures Consequences: International Differences in Work-Related Values.* Beverley Hills: Sage Publications.

Hofstede, G. (1984). *Culture's Consequences.* Newbury: Sage Publications.

Hofstede, G. (1997).*Software of the Mind: Intercultural Cooperation and its Importance for Survival.* New York: McGraw Hill.

Hofstede, G., and Bond, M.H. (1988).'The Confucius Connection: From Cultural Roots to Economic Growth'. *Organizational Dynamics, 16,*4, pp. 4-21.

Holden, G. (2006). 'Integrating and embedding employability.' In, Becket, N. and Kemp, P. (eds.). *Enhancing graduate employability in business and management, hospitality, leisure, sport, tourism.*Newbury: Threshold.

Holmes, L. (2001). 'Reconsidering graduate employability: the 'graduate identity' approach.' *Quality in Higher Education,7,2*, pp. 111-119.

Holtbrugge, D. (2010). 'Cultural determinants of learning style preference.' *Academy of Management Learning & Education.9,* 4, pp. 622-637.

Hosford, C. and Siders, W. (2010). 'Felder-Soloman's Index of Learning Styles': Internal Consistency, Temporal Stability, and Factor Structure'. *Teaching and Learning in Medicine, 22,4*, pp. 298-303.

Jackson, N. (2011). *Learning for a complex world.A lifewide concept of learning, education and personal development.* Bloomington: Author House.

Johnson, S. and Burden, T. (2003).*Young people, employability and the induction process.* York: Joseph Rowntree Foundation.

Jusdanis, G. (1995). 'Beyond national culture?',*Boundary, 22*, pp. 23-59.

Kang, F. and Song, G. (2007). 'e-Learning in Higher Education in China.' In H.Spencer-Oatey (ed), *e-Learning Initiatives in China.* Hong Kong: Hong Kong University Press.

Khanna, T, (2008). *Billions of Entrepreneurs in China and India: How China and India are reshaping their futures and yours.* Boston: Harvard Business School.

Knight, P. (2001).'Editorial: Employability and quality', *Quality in Higher Education, 7,2*, pp. 93-95.

Knight, P., and Yorke, M. (2004).*Learning, Curriculum and Employability in Higher Education,* London:Routledge/Falmer.

Kolb, D. A. (1996).*Learning-Styles Inventory: Self-Scoring Test and Interpretation Booklet.* Boston: Hat/McBer Training Resources Group.

Kroeber, A. L. and Kluckholn, C. (1952).*Culture: A critical review of concepts and definitions;Anthropological paper no. 4,* Cambridge (MA): Peabody Museum.

Ladd, P.D, and Ruby, R. (1999).'Learning style and adjustment Issues of international students',*Journal of Education for Business,* July/August, pp. 363-367.

Law, B. and Watts, A.G. (1977).*Schools, careers and community.* London: Church Information Office.

Lee, W.O. (1996). 'The Cultural Context for the Asian Learners: Conceptions of Learning in the Confucian Tradition', In, Watkins, D.and Biggs, J. (eds.), *The Chinese Learner: Cultural, Psychological and Contextual Influences.* Hong Kong: Comparative Education Research Centre, University of Hong Kong.

Li,Y., Liu, S., and Wong, S. (2005).'The influences on employment quality from employability', *Higher Education Exploration, 2,* pp. 91-93.

Little, B. (2006).*Employability and work-based learning.* Learning and Employability Series: ESECT.

Liu, M., and Zoninsein, M. [online] (2007). 'These Surfers Do It Their Own Way.' *Newsweek*. Available at: http://www.newsweek.com/id/78112. Accessed 26.06.09.

Liu, J. and Zhang, X. (2008).'Research on reforming higher education pattern to develop employability', *Social Science Journal of Colleges of Shanxi, 20,3,* pp. 124-126.

Liu, J. Nie, J., and Qiu, H. (2008). 'Exploring strategy for enhancing college students' employability', *Education Research Monthly, 10,* pp. 52-55.

Luo, H., Li, R. and Wang, H. (2011). *Chinese College Graduates' Employment: Annual Report.* Beijing: MyCos.

Manzoor, S. [online] (2010). 'Ready and able; Should universities teach students how to find a job?.' Available at: http://www.guardian.co.uk/education/2010/jul/27/graduate-job-crisis Accessed: 1.12.11.

Mao. (2008).'An analysis of the changes of the scale in China's higher education.',*Statistics research, 25,*3, pp. 55-59.

Ministry of Education (MOE), [online] (2008). 'Various.' Available at: www.moe.edu.cn. Accessed: 5.12.11.

Moreland, N. (2005). *Work related learning in Higher Education.* London: The Higher Education Academy.

Mu, L. (2006).'Exploring the approaches to train students' employability', *China Graduates Employment, 16,* pp. 8-9.

Nakata, C., and Sivakuma, K. (2001). 'Instituting the Marketing Concept in a Multinational Setting: The Role of National Culture'. *Journal of the Academy of Marketing Science, 29,*3,pp. 336-346.

National Bureau of Statistics of P.R. China, (2001).*China Statistical Yearbook 2001.*Beijing: China Statistics Press.

NCIHE, (1997).*Employability: Higher Education and Career Services: The Dearing Report.* Norwich, HMSO.

Oldfield, B.M, and Baron, S. (2000), 'Student perceptions of service quality in a UK university business and management faculty', *Quality Assurance in Education, 8,*2, pp. 85-95.

Pascarella, E. T., and Terenzini, P. T. (1991). *How college affects students: Findings and insights from twenty years of research.* San Francisco: Jossey-Bass.

Petrova, P. and Ujma, D. (2006).'Students' awareness of the importance of transferable skills for employability.' In, Becket, N. and Kemp, P. (eds.). *Enhancing graduate employability in business and management, hospitality, leisure, sport and tourism.* Norfolk: Threshold.

References

Plymouth University.[online] (2011). 'Work experience'. Available at: http://www.plymouth.ac.uk/pages/view.asp?page=31613. Accessed: 1.11.11.

Pratt, D.P. (1991).'Conceptions of self within China and the Unites States: Contrasting foundations for adult education', *International Journal of Intercultural Relations, 15,* pp. 285-310.

Raybould, J. and Sheedy, V. (2005). 'Are graduates equipped with the right skills in the employability stakes?' *Industrial and Commercial Training.37,* 5, pp. 259-263.

Rees, G., Gorard, S., Fevre, R. and Furlong, J. (1997). 'History, Place and the Learning Society: towards a sociology of lifetime learning.' *Journal of Education Policy, 12*, 6, pp. 485-497.

Reichman, S., and Grasha, A.F. (1974).,A rational approach to developing and assessing the construct validity of a student learning scale instrument.'*Journal of Psychology, 87*, pp. 213-223.

Rivas-Drake, D. (2008). 'Perceived opportunity, ethnic identity, and achievement motivation among Latinos at a selective public university.'*Journal of Latinos and Education, 7, 2,* 113-128.

Robotham, D. (1999). 'The Application of learning Style Theory in Higher Education Teaching.', Available at:http://www.chelt.ac.uk/el/philg/gdn/discuss/kolb2.htm. Accessed: 10.9.01.

Rodrigues, C.A., Bu, N., and Min, B. (2000).'Learners' training approach preference: National culture as a determinant', *Cross Cultural Management - an International Journal, 7,*1, pp. 23-32.

Rundle-Thiele, S., Bennett, R., Dann, S. (2005). 'The Successful Preparation and Development of Future Marketing Professionals: A Recommended Methodological Framework.' *Journal of Advancement of Marketing Education,7,* pp. 27-35.

Salili, F. (1996).'Accepting personal responsibility for learning', In Watkins D. and Biggs J. (eds.), *The Chinese learner: Cultural, psychological and contextual influences.* Hong Kong: CERC and Melbourne: ACER.

Schudson, M. (1994).'Culture and the integration of national societies.'*International Social Science Journal, 46,* pp. 63-81.

Shu, X. (1961).*The Statistics of China's modern education.Beijing:* People's education press.

Smith, P. J. (2001). 'Technology Student Learning Preferences and the Design of Flexible Learning Programs.'*Instructional Science,29,* pp. 237-254.

Soloman, B. A. and Felder, R. M., (2002).,Index of Learning Styles.'Available from http://www.ncsu.edu/felder-public/ILSpage.html. Accessed 01.03.06.

State Council: China. (2004). *The 2003-2007 Action Plan for Invigorating Education,* Beijing: China.

Sweeney, A., Morrison, M., Jarratt, D. and Heffernan, T. (2009). 'Modelling the constructs contributing to the effectiveness of Marketing lecturers.' *Journal of Marketing Education.31*, 3, pp. 190-202.

Tomlinson, M. (2008). 'The degree is not enough': students' perceptions of the role of higher education credentials for graduate work and employability'. *British Journal of Sociology of Education.29,*1, pp. 49-61.

Tse, E. (2010). 'Is it too late to enter China', *Harvard Business Review,* April 2010.

UK National Committee of Inquiry into Higher Education (the Dearing Committee) (1997a), *Higher Education in the Learning Society: Summary Report,* London: HMSO.

Universities UK (UUK). (2007). *Beyond the honours degree classification: the Burgess Group Final Report.* London: UUK.

Universities UK, (2008).Available at: http://www.universitiesuk.ac.uk/Pages/ Default.aspx.Accessed: 23.1.10.

United Nations. (2008). *Creative Report: The Challenges of Assessing the Creative Economy; towards informed Policy Making;* Available at: http:// www.unctad.org/en/docs/ditc20082cer_en.pdf Accessed: 2.12.11.

UniversitiesUK (2011).Patterns and Trends in UK Higher Education. Available at: http://www.UniversitiesUK.ac.uk/Publications/Documents/PatternsAndT rendsinUKHigherEducation.pdf.Accessed: 25.10.11.

Venter, K. (2003).'Building on formal education: employers' approaches to the training and development of new recruits in the People's Republic of China', *International Journal of Training and Development, 7*,3, pp.186-202.

Villeneuve-Smith, M., Marshall, F., and McKenzie, E. (2008).*Employability Skills Explored*, London: Learning and Skills Network (LSN)

Vitae, [online] (2009). 'Research destinations, What do researchers do?' Available at: http://www.vitae.ac.uk/CMS/files/upload/Vitae-WDRD-by-subject-Jun-09.pdf Accessed: 2.12.11.

Wallace, A. F. (1970). *Culture and Personality.*New York: Random House.

Welch, A. (1997), 'The peripatetic professor: the internationalisation of the academic profession,' *Higher Education, 34,* 6, pp. 323-45.

Wellman, N. (2010a). 'The employability attributes required of new marketing graduates.' *Marketing Intelligence & Planning.28*,7, pp. 908-930.

Wellman, N. (2010b). 'Relating the curriculum to marketing competence: a conceptual framework.'*The Marketing Review.10,* 2, pp. 119-134.

Wen, S. (2006), 'A research on the development strategies of graduate employability and the cultivation of talents', *Modern University Education, 1,* pp. 101-108.

Wickramasinghe, V. and Perera, L. (2010). 'Graduates', university lecturers' and employers' perceptions towards employability skills', *Education + Training, 52*, 3, pp.226 - 244.

Williams, M. (2003).*Making sense of social research.*London: Sage.

Williams, M and Vogt, P (eds) (2011). *Sage Handbook of Methodological Innovation.* London: Sage.

Wratcher, M. A., Morrison, E. E., Riley, V.L., and Scheirton, L. S. (1997). *Curriculum and program planning: A study guide for the core seminar.* Programs for higher education: Nova Southeastern University.

Wu, Y. and Luo, G. (2011). 'Choice of employability; development of universities' students.' *China University Teaching. 5*, pp. 75-77.

Xiao, Z. and Dyson, J.R. (1999).'Chinese students' perceptions of good accounting teaching.'*Accounting Education, 8,* 4, pp. 341-61.

Yamazaki, Y. (2005). 'Learning styles and typologies of cultural differences: A theoretical and empirical comparison.' *International Journal of Intercultural Relations. 29*, pp. 521-548.

Yorke, M. (2004).*Employability in Higher Education: What It Is - What It Is Not, Learning and Employability Series.* London: The Higher Education Academy.

Yorke, M., and Knight, P. (2007) 'Evidence-informed pedagogy and the enhancement of student employability.' *Teaching in Higher Education. 12,* 2, pp. 157-170.

Young, T. (2010). 'How valid and useful is the notion of learning style? A multicultural investigation.' *Procedia Social and Behavioral Sciences. 2,* pp. 427-433.

Yuan X. (2008).'The enrolment of higher education reaches a new historical peak.' Available at: http://edu.qq.com /a/20080507/000013.htm. Accessed: 10.12.08.

Zeng, X. (2004). 'Job seeking of college graduates in employment environment under transition.' *Economic Research Journal. 6,* pp. 87-95.

Zhang, Y. (2006).'Social occupational classes and higher-education opportunities in contemporary China: A study on the distributional of a scarce social capital', *Front. Educ, China, 1*, pp. 89-99.

Zhang, Q. and Zhao, L. (2007). 'Reasons, social influence and solutions of difficulty of graduates' employment. *Modern Education Management. 4.*

Zheng, Y., Jin, Y., Sun, Y., and Jiao, F. (2008).'Build up the course system to enhance the level of employability', *Hei Long Jiang Education, 3*, pp. 60-91.

Zhiwen, G., and van der Heijden, B. (2008). 'Employability enhancement of business graduates in China: Reacting upon challenges of globalization and labour market demands', *Education & Training, 50,4,* pp. 289-304.

Zou, Q. (2011). 'How to improve the employability of vocational college students. *Management Observer. 2,* pp. 128-129.